The Soul of a New Self

Embracing the Future of Being Human

JEFF CARREIRA

Jeff Carreira

The Soul of a New Self:
Embracing the Future of Being Human
By Jeff Carreira

Copyright © 2016 Jeff Carreira

ISBN-13: 978-0692453070
ISBN-10: 0692453075

Published by Emergence Education Press
Philadelphia, PA 19147

Cover Design by www.choosefreeagency.com

Jeff Carreira

With this book, Jeff Carreira has done something extraordinary. He employs the philosophy of the American pragmatists as an interpretive framework for his own deeply coherent mystical experiences, and in the process opens up completely new possibilities for philosophy and contemplative practices. This is a work of discovery and invention, of observation and imagination, of intellect and embodied perception. Jeff has developed a unique and delightful narrative style, weaving a new kind of inquiry he calls "wormholing" with a personal account of his own journey and aspirations. His personal story draws us in as intimate partners in a deeply holistic universe of lived experience. His invitation to "wormhole" with him helps us to examine the assumptions that underlie the metaphysical foundations of our existing paradigm that constrain all our current worldviews. This is as challenging as pointing out water to a fish—and yet Jeff guides us through his thought experiments with natural language and playful prodding. This gives us the opportunity to see the world through his enlightened eyes and experience his expansion of the ordinary self into a far greater possibility than we could ever know.

Bonnitta Roy, Founder of Alderlore Insight Center
Associate Editor, Integral Review Journal
Program Coordinator, MA in Consciousness Studies, the Graduate
Institute

The Soul of a New Self explores the most vital question of our time: Who are we? Jeff Carreira's passionate quest and response to this question moves me deeply. He describes his recognition that "I," the being that I am right now, is the universe awakening to its own existence. Yet it is also true that the individual self is an expression of the universe in unique form. I love this book. It is worthy of true dialogue among us. I hope you will read it and that we will explore it together.

Barbara Marx Hubbard, author of *Conscious Evolution* and
founder of The Foundation for Conscious Evolution

v

This book is subversive. It offers the reader, step by step, nothing less than a new way of imagining our very identity. It is a radical inquiry into some long-held cultural assumptions about the nature of self, and the filters we place on reality that limit our capacity to see what's in front of our eyes. The result transcends arid, rational thinking. It is what the perennial traditions call wisdom, reflecting the heart of a true mystic. Reading this book carefully results in a transformation of consciousness.

Bruce Sanguin, author of
Jesus and the Evolving Mystic: The Path of Love

In The Soul of a New Self *Jeff Carreira weaves together a rich tapestry of wisdom traditions from the silken threads of figures like Ralph Waldo Emerson, Teilhard de Chardin, Sri Aurobindo, the American philosophy of pragmatism and the Indian philosophy of Advaita Vedanta, in a sweeping textual vision of the new human potentials that appear to be emerging through our countless and varied mystical experiences. Of particular note are the author's own spiritual realizations that reveal the deep experiential well from which this particular text was written. The result is another shining example of America's mystical democracy and religion of no religion.*

Jeffrey J. Kripal, author of
Esalen: America and the Religion of No Religion

The Soul of a New Self *encourages us to question our assumptions of separation and isolation so that we can embrace the deeper harmony that connects us all. With humor, intelligence and grace Jeff reveals why our current separate sense of individual identity is not the totality of who we are. In these pages you will encounter a profound vision of how deeply connected you are to all of life, and catch the vision of a dramatically different possibility for human experience.*

Katherine Woodward Thomas, author of
Conscious Uncoupling: 5 Steps to Living Happily Even After

In *Soul of a New Self*, Jeff Carreira guides us past the illusion of separation, and into the foundational consciousness of a new way of being. The book brings us to the edge of who we have known ourselves to be, individually and as a species, and opens us to possibilities of transcendence. This profoundly absorbing work ushers in the 'First Light' of a new Spiritual Paradigm that is awakening from the ground of our Being. Jeff's potent experience in spiritual mysticism and profound sensitivity to the deeper blossoming of consciousness opens us to a precipice of illumination. The Soul of a New Self is a beacon guiding us towards an awakened world beyond our imagination.

Jody Mountain, Lineage of Light

Jeff Carreira shows the false assumptions underlying our conventional self-sense and what happens when those false assumptions are removed from the experience of who we are. The result is a fundamental change in consciousness. Since culture is based on consciousness—specifically, the prevailing mode of consciousness that dominates a society—The Soul of a New Self offers insights and guidelines for the emergence of a higher human culture, based on a significant number of people who have changed their consciousness from self-centered to Being- centered.

John White, author of
Meeting of Science and Spirit: Guidelines for a New Age
and *Kundalini, Evolution and Enlightenment*

This is an important book. In writing this Jeff Carreira is prompting us not only to find our individual enlightenment, not only to seek enlightenment collectively, not even to open ourselves to a higher source of wisdom, but to escape the limitations of our dimensionality and actually recognize the relational field as a being. Then to see not only that "I am that" but also we all are that, and "that", now and forever, is the soul of the new Self.

Dr. Jeffrey Eisen, author of *Oneness Perceived* and founder of
The PsychoNoetics Science Institute

Jeff Carreira

ACKNOWLEDGEMENTS

I want to thank a few of the many people who have supported me through the writing of this book.

My wife Amy Edelstein, who is my constant companion and the source of so much of the Wisdom that I have to share.

My spiritual brother and teaching partner Craig Hamilton, whose advice and support has been invaluable to my work.

To my former teacher Andrew Cohen, who initiated me on the path of awakening.

To Patricia Albere, who shared so much of herself with me during the time that we worked together.

To Jill Ouellette for her generous editorial support and many insightful conversations during the writing of this book.

To all the baristas at the *Milk & Honey* café on 4th Street in Philadelphia, where I wrote most of this book.

And to countless others who have and continue to support everything I do. Thank you.

Jeff Carreira

CONTENTS

Foreword   i

Introduction   1

1   Multi-Dimensional Consciousness   9

2   The Non-Locality of Self   35

3   The Implications of Being a Being   59

4   The Thinking-Thing Self   81

5   Committed to Being Me   103

6   The Human Flow   125

7   Redistributing the Self   149

8   You Can't Be Here and There   175

9   Embracing a New Self   201

FOREWORD
By Craig Hamilton

Many of us alive today are excited about the emergence of a new, more unitive paradigm. Weary of the collective pain wrought by eons of dualistic and divisive thinking, we long for a new world organized around the truth of our essential unity or oneness—a world, in short, fundamentally moved by love.

This enthusiasm for unity is certainly cause for optimism. As more and more of us connect in this shared longing, our confidence in its validity grows stronger, its current gains momentum and our shared commitment to its emergence solidifies.

But, as Jeff Carreira illuminates in the pages that follow, it is one thing to be inspired by the idea of Oneness and quite another to surrender to its life-altering implications.

For those of us who feel called to end the failed paradigm of separation, the question Jeff asks us is: are we ready to leave behind not only the world as we have known it until now, but the very person we have known ourselves to be? If we want to live in a world unified in the truth of Oneness, are we willing to give up our investment in the edifice of autonomy we've spent a lifetime erecting and defending?

As the title suggests, this is a book about the self. But the self the author is referring to is not anything like any self most of us have ever encountered.

This book is about the emergence of a self without boundaries, a self uncontained by the identity constructs of the mind, a self so vast that it ultimately includes all of us, or at least all of us willing to allow ourselves to be included within it. And it includes much more than that too.

You are holding in your hands an unusual book, and as such it defies conventional description. It is at once a philosophical treatise, a spiritual guidebook, and a reflection on a life of intense contemplative practice.

As I've spent time with its pages, I've also come to think of *The Soul of a New Self* as a message from the future, an invitation from an intrepid explorer who has dared to leave behind the familiar and explore the leading edges of humanity's next evolutionary stage.

Although this book is primarily a philosophical exploration, its message is not one derived from merely thinking about ideas. It is philosophy rooted in the direct experience of a dimension of reality that lies beyond conceptualization. And, in this case, a dimension of reality that lies beyond individuality itself.

The experiences that served as the foundation for this

book were not mystical experiences in the usual sense, because they were not the experiences of a single individual. They were collective experiences—discoveries of a group of spiritual explorers who, in an unusual evolutionary experiment, tried to venture into awakened consciousness together.

Fifteen years ago, in a collective spiritual exploration at the far reaches of the known, the author found himself awakening to a radical truth that would leave him unrecognizable to the self he had known up to that point.

That radical truth was not only that reality is one or that consciousness is unified, but that it is possible for a group of dedicated human beings to consciously discover and be animated by that single unified consciousness—together. It is possible, in other words, to awaken as a collective.

I'm writing this because I had the privilege to be part of that collective. In the summer of 2001, along with fourteen fellow spiritual astronauts, Jeff and I embarked on a unique kind of retreat that ultimately propelled us into an unexpected awakening.

Like many retreats, ours was structured around several hours each day of intensive silent meditation plumbing the depths of Being. But several times each day, we would also break from our meditation to discuss what was awakening within us. It was in one such discussion that the miraculous happened.

As we sat in a circle stretching to give voice to the mysteries that were unveiling themselves in our meditation, it was as if the seemingly solid boundaries between us began to dissolve. As each person spoke in turn, the experience of unity intensified until the very perception of separation itself had given way to a single seamless field of experience. Where there once had been a group of apparently distinct individuals, now there was a single being.

If you've done much spiritual practice, you've likely experienced moments or even extended periods of perceptual unity in which the world and all the seemingly solid objects in it melted into an indivisible flow of energy. And that was certainly a part of what unfolded between us that summer afternoon. But there was something else afoot that day that ultimately proved to be of much greater significance.

What happened between us that day was not simply a group of individuals having a shared mystical experience. It was a single awakened consciousness having an experience of being a group of individuals.

Put another way, it was the experience of being a single self, a single being, alive in many bodies, animating a group of minds and hearts, looking out through fifteen pairs of eyes.

Individuality didn't disappear. But the identity structure most of us take for granted was nowhere to be found.

And somehow, in the vacuum left in its place, a new self was able to arise to fill the void. And as it emerged, it began to take on a life of its own.

For what ultimately became much more significant than the cosmic experience we shared in that circle was the life this new collective awakened self began to live beyond the walls of that room. As we each went on carrying about with our lives, something was different. There seemed to be a new self living through us—a self no longer confined to our individual bodies, our personal life histories, or our unique identities.

This new self pulsed with the energy of Love; it contained the truth of Oneness; and yet it was also alive with the reality of we-ness and even I-ness. It was not just a Higher Self that knows our ultimate non-separateness. It was an individuated experience of wholeness that at once contained everything born and unborn and yet found its life only in each unique individual perspective willing to surrender to its immensity.

If what I'm trying to describe sounds unnecessarily esoteric or a bit too sci-fi for comfort, that's probably because I am challenged to find a way to put something so unusual into words.

Indeed, it has been precisely this endeavor to find a way to articulate the radical unitive worldview and way of being that this self brings with it that ultimately led to the creation of this book you now hold in your hands. In the pages that follow, Jeff Carreira will share with you his own attempt to make the incomprehensible a bit more comprehensible, to bring at least one experience of heaven down to earth that we might all be elevated by our encounter with it.

As you engage with the message of this book, I invite you to try a little experiment: try to allow yourself to *not know* who is reading the book. I'm not suggesting you should reject or relinquish your current beliefs about the self or your current experience of being yourself. But I am suggesting that if you can temporarily suspend any certainty about what a self is or who *your* self is, you will have the best chance of catching a glimpse of the new self Jeff is describing.

For, in what may be the most encouraging truth of all,

once a new self is born—even a collective self—it takes on a life of its own, and because this life transcends any individual's experience of it, we can all partake in its ongoing emergence.

This new self has already emerged. It is here right now. It is the self that is writing these words, and it is likely that it might also be the self reading these words.

Whether or not you have any direct experience of it, the reality of Oneness has always been the only true reality there is. No matter how separate or distinct any of us might feel or appear on any given day, there has only ever been a single consciousness having that experience.

Because Unity is already the case, its knowledge is not something that needs to be cultivated or developed. We only need give up our habitual insistence on separation.

As you read the pages that follow, it is my hope therefore that you will at some point take the risk to release any mental argument with the words on the page and allow yourself to be swept up in the current of awakening that is flowing between the lines.

Finding the courage to awaken has always been a revolutionary act, and now, with the emergence of the soul of a new self, it is an evolutionary one as well. As each of us relinquishes who we have taken ourselves to be for who we can know ourselves to be together, we are creating the very unified new world our hearts most deeply long for.

And when enough of us say yes to this possibility, we will have created heaven on earth.

The misconception which has haunted philosophic literature throughout the centuries is the notion of 'independent existence.' There is no such mode of existence; every entity is to be understood in terms of the way it is interwoven with the rest of the universe.

Alfred North Whitehead

INTRODUCTION

The book you are about to read is an exploration of the meaning and significance of a remarkable form of spiritual experience that more and more people seem to be having these days. It is an experience that is often called collective, or inter-subjective awakening.

For many years I lived in a spiritual community that was largely focused on doing whatever it took to generate an awakening that was not limited to the experience of a single individual, but was collectively held by many people at once.

After nearly a decade of pursuit that culminated in eight months of intensively focused practice I had the privilege of being present during an explosive awakening of a small group of individuals.

To be clear, this collective awakening is not a group of individuals experiencing illumination separately, but at the same time. This was an awakening of a group of separate individuals to a single consciousness that was animating each of them. This higher mind was speaking the words that emerged from each person's mouth, thinking the thoughts in each person's mind, and feeling the emotions that arose in every individual's heart. It was a singular source of being that was living through a group of individuals.

Although I had spent years preparing for this possibility, there was no way to be ready for it. It was utterly incomprehensible and totally undeniable at the same time. In that group I could see that everyone's eyes were looking at me from the same place that I was looking at them. I could hear that the words they spoke came from a shared intelligence that had become the source of my consciousness. And when I felt something I saw that it washed through everyone in the room as if we shared one body and one nervous system.

The rules of being had been completely rewritten. I not only had no idea who I was; I didn't know what I was, or even if I was. Everything was different. It was like landing on the surface of a new world, and everywhere you looked there was more to discover.

What did it mean about being human, about our evolutionary potential, and about the future of our world?

Over a few week's time we remained in this collectively awakened space, and we looked into all these questions and many more. That event occurred in the summer of 2001, and it cemented my raison d'être. From that time on my life has been primarily dedicated to understanding and facilitating collective awakening. I want to understand that experience and its implications so that I can make it intelligible and available to others.

This book is an attempt to do just that.

You won't find a detailed description of the experience I just mentioned until the very last chapter of this book. I did this on purpose because I wanted to use all of the earlier chapters to create the right context for that experience to land in. Some of my early readers felt it might be useful to know where I was going from the start so in the end I decided to say something about it right here in the introduction.

Now before you dive into the first chapter there are a few more things I want you to know about this book and how I've structured it. It is part philosophical, part mystical, and part personal, weaving freely through explication, revelation, and anecdote. I suggest you read it as poetry or literature because this will create space and allow something more than the facts and information to come through its pages. There is plenty of knowledge to be gained here, but if all you get from these pages is knowledge, my true intentions will not be served.

The power of literature is found in the effect of the piece as a whole. Take for instance Ken Kesey's great novel *Sometimes a Great Notion*. The story is an epic tale of an Oregon logging family told from multiple first-person perspectives. I read the book many years ago, and I still remember distinctly the feeling that descended over me as I read the dramatic final scene.

I was sitting outside on a warm summer evening looking up at the stars. After closing the book, I spent a few minutes just letting the full impact of the story wash over me. All of the characters I had gotten to know so well and all the tragedy and triumph that had befallen them came together in a final crescendo of meaningfulness.

Something about the delicacy of the human condition had been communicated. The transmission was not literal and explicit. It occurred in the afterglow of the story's completion. During those few moments I became intimately acquainted with myself. The drama of life came starkly into focus, leaving me with a deep sense of the enormity of the reality within which I exist but often remain unaware of.

I realized that the whole novel, all 640 pages, had been written for this moment of recognition and realization. Each word was a domino arranged in an intricate pattern. In the final pages the last domino was knocked over, initiating a wave that rippled back through my memory of the story, revealing a secret that could not be experienced until the end. I was flooded with gratitude for the author's willingness to share this moment with me.

I cannot claim to have anything like the literary skill of a genius like Ken Kesey, but I do encourage you to read this book like literature or poetry, keeping in mind that it is pointing toward a possibility that is contained in the whole, not in any of the pieces held in isolation.

In this way the book is a good metaphor for the new paradigm that it attempts to elucidate. The fundamental insight being communicated is that the assumption of separation that the Western world has lived inside of for nearly four centuries is inaccurate. During the Enlightenment era we learned to separate ourselves from reality. We sought a detached and dispassionate vantage point from which to see things more clearly. We learned to experience ourselves as subjects viewing objects that were separate from us. The miraculous blessings of modern science and the world that it created were the result.

Now we are experiencing the limitations of this overly fragmented and objectified perception of reality. We find ourselves unable to cope with the size, scope, and complexity of the challenges we face. At the very same time, many of us have experienced a different, more holistic perception of reality and recognize it to be the arrival of the new paradigm that is needed.

The new paradigm will be based on an assumption of oneness and continuity. It will live in the recognition that there is nothing ultimately separating anything from anything else. The entirety of reality will not be experienced as a collection of objects, but rather as one living continuously unfolding being.

This book presents visions, images, and conclusions that are born out of experiences beyond the current paradigm. It challenges assumptions and beliefs that are held so deeply in our psyche that they have become inseparable from our experience of reality itself. Exposing these assumptions creates a space in which the seeds of a new paradigm can be planted and grow in our being.

This book is particularly focused on that elusive thing called a "self." We are profoundly identified with the experience of selfhood. We believe that we are the self that we experience ourselves to be. Our conscious awareness is shaped by our sense of self, but that sense of self is not who we are. As long as we believe that we are only the self that we experience ourselves to be, our life energy remains trapped inside the experience of that self.

A new paradigm necessitates a new sense of self to occupy it. This book invites you to allow your current sense of identity to be gently displaced, giving a new self the opportunity to reveal itself. This new self is not an isolated individual thinking thing. It is an expansive, unlimited, collective being that we will grow into together as One.

Writing about a new paradigm is like trying to see the backside of your eyeballs. The paradigm we exist in is the invisible conceptual background that makes everything else intelligible but is itself incomprehensible. Like the wind, you can't see it directly. You only see evidence of it. Blowing leaves, bending branches, people bending forward as they walk, are all indicators of the existence of a breeze that you cannot see. Similarly, to beings like us, embedded as we are in the paradigm of separation, the new paradigm of continuity only reveals itself in glimpses and fleeting bursts of revelation.

The first three chapters of this book give a high-altitude overview of the terrain to be explored. Chapter one offers a multi-dimensional explanation of reality as a way of understanding the origin of mystical experiences. Chapter two expands our conception of self beyond the customary boundaries of time and of isolated existence. The third chapter introduces profound moral considerations involved in redefining the self for a new age.

The remaining six chapters of the book take the reader through a detailed contemplation of our current sense of self and finally into speculations about what the next evolution of selfhood might be. Chapters four and five illuminate structures of the self that we currently live inside of and offers a theoretical exploration to help us understand how we actively participate in creating and maintaining these structures.

Chapter six is a turning point. It presents considerations on the nature of reality that eliminate the necessity of assuming the existence of any self whatsoever. Entertaining the possibility of no-self creates the space within which a new sense of self has room to grow.

Chapters seven and eight begin the process of reconceiving the self in terms that allow us to see ourselves beyond assumed limitations of embodied existences. The final chapter is the most personal. In it I describe some of my deepest experiences of a new self and offer conclusions about who we are and how we can re-create ourselves.

As you read these pages, please hold your mind wide open, allowing the words to wash over you fully. Let the images, metaphors, stories, and philosophical arguments move fluidly across the expanse of your consciousness like clouds in the sky.

I remember lying on my back as a child looking up at the clouds. They would move and change shape— sometimes combining, sometimes separating, constantly in subtle motion. Occasionally a distinct image would emerge—a lion, a train, or a person. The figure would appear distinct and clear for a time before returning to the puffy mass of water vapor that it was before.

Reading with childlike curiosity and imagination will allow the unusual nature of the writing to come to life in bursts of insight and recognition designed to provoke you into a deeper understanding of who you are and who we will become.

CHAPTER ONE

MULTI-DIMENSIONAL
CONSCIOUSNESS

The premise of this book is that the soul of a new self is forming in consciousness and we have the opportunity to participate in its birth. In fact we are already answering the call of that possibility. Much of what we are being drawn toward, perhaps even reading this book, is an answer to that call. You see, a new soul begins as an attractive energy that appears in the mysterious space of awareness. Currently there is an attractive energy gathering some of us together in a process of unification and harmonization that will stabilize into a new way of being. The curiosity you felt to read this book is a manifestation of that energy. Whatever has compelled you forward on your transformative journey is also that energy. Something is calling us together, and that something is the energy associated with the soul of a new self.

The form of the new way of being is unimaginable, and I mean that literally. This book is about the possibility of becoming a different kind of human being, and the person we are now cannot imagine what that will be like. Luckily we sometimes have intuitions and visions that take us beyond ourselves. Those precious glimpses into the unimaginable allow us to piece together ideas, perspectives, and practices that inspire and support us along the way.

This process of unification and self-creation is not just happening in human beings because it is not only human consciousness that is evolving. In fact any understanding of this transformation has to start with the recognition that consciousness is not the possession of an individual or species. Consciousness is not something that is inside of us. We are inside of it. Those of us who are concerned about the evolution of consciousness can't help thinking about it in human terms because the human experience of consciousness is all we have access to. This leads to a bias toward human consciousness over other forms of consciousness in our thinking. This perfectly understandable tendency will be reconfigured and corrected for in the new way of being. Human beings will offer a unique expression of the new being but not the only one and perhaps not even the most important one.

The shift that we are exploring in this book will lead to a new way of being that will reconfigure everything. I am even hesitant to draw upon current theories of evolution because they are also rooted in our current conceptions of time, space, and being and are destined to be reconfigured themselves. Imagine trying to build an intricately designed ship that could sail successfully over the edge of a flat earth only to discover that the earth is round. Every age creates its own set of elaborate theories to explain the way things are, and every next age begins with the discovery that everything is different than we had thought.

What this book calls into question is our current understanding of ourselves. We have been deeply conditioned to see ourselves as separate entities, housed in separate bodies, living a single lifetime in a world that is independent from us. We have been taught that we have consciousness inside of us and that our brains gather information from the world outside and form pictures of reality that allow us to know things. This is the currently dominant experience of being human, and the experience of the next level of being lies beyond our ability to imagine. To approach a possibility that is unimaginable we must engage in a profoundly open-ended inquiry. We must ask questions without settling on answers. I believe that unrestricted receptivity is the key to participating in the evolution of consciousness.

To embark on an inquiry this broad we need to think deeply about how we think. When you want to understand something, what do you do? Generally we try to see what it is made of. We have been taught to assume that distinctions create understanding. When one thing is seen to include two or more parts, we have gained some information about the thing. This way of acquiring knowledge could be called dualistic thinking. When we think dualistically, we look for divisions. We understand things by separating them into parts.

This way of thinking is often referred to as reductionist—although when we call someone a reductionist we are also implying that they believe that the whole of something can be reduced to the sum of its parts. As I am using these terms, not all dualistic thinking has to be reductionist. You can understand something by splitting it into parts and still know that the whole is more than just those parts. We can appreciate and use the wisdom of dualistic thinking without limiting everything to it.

This book will argue against the reductionist position, but even more interesting it will suggest the possibility of going beyond all forms of dualistic thinking. That means not only seeing beyond the assumption that wholes are merely the sums of parts, but also seeing through the illusion that anything is separate from anything else. It is a holistic form of thinking that is so far beyond the way we have been trained to think that we cannot get to it through the dualistic processing system that we are currently operating within. Glimpses of the world beyond dualism come to us in flashes of insight and episodes of spiritual realization. These are leaps in perception that are as mysterious as the visions of reality they open into.

There are certain spiritual practices and forms of inquiry that create fertile ground for these spontaneous shifts in awareness. The contemplation of the nature of consciousness and the existence of self is one such inquiry and the focus of this book. What we will find is that to go beyond dualistic thinking and assumptions of separation we must go beyond our culture's most commonly accepted models of mind.

Most of us have been taught to understand mind, thought, and self through a dualistic model of reality. I call that model of reality things-in-space consciousness, and it was born in the West during the time period known as the Enlightenment. Over the course of about two centuries we moved out of the worldview of the Middle Ages and into the Modern Era. During this transition, objectivity was prized. We learned to separate ourselves from nature. We began to see ourselves as independent, thinking beings with minds that were perfectly constructed to uncover nature's secrets and understand the mechanisms of creation.

The birth of the Modern Age brought with it the birth of a self that saw itself as limited to a single lifetime and existing within an individual body in a dance of interaction with other independent entities. We came to believe that our minds and our seemingly limitless power of rationality made us unique among all of nature's other creations. A separation between self and other was etched so deep in the field of consciousness that the bottom of the trench went too far down to see. Looking down at that seemingly bottomless divide we lost touch with the deeper connection between us. Like a flower that doesn't see its own roots, we fell into a dream of separation that cut us off where the stem meets the ground. This fundamental assumption of separation colors all of our perceptions, especially our perception of our self and the source of our awareness.

Seeing ourselves as fundamentally separate, we naturally assume that the capacity for consciousness that we experience lives inside of us. And in our scientifically informed age we most likely imagine that consciousness resides in our brain and even more that it is a product of brain activity. We have learned that through our senses we take in information about the world and believe that our brain compiles that information into an experience of reality. We experience the world like a movie on a mental screen.

What if this were not true? As I look out at the other people in this coffee shop, my habit is to assume that they all contain a source of consciousness separate from mine. Each of them is a self—a being with a consciousness-producing brain or what I like to call a thinking-thing. If we experience reality in terms of things-in-space, then we see ourselves as thinking-things.

What would an alternative view look like? What else could we be if not a thinking-thing?

The alternative view that we will explore in this book is that a self is not an independently conscious entity. A self, as my friend and colleague Dr. Jeffrey Eisen puts it, is a platform of perception. It is not a something that sees; it is a place to see from. I believe, as the American philosopher William James did, that reality is created from pure experience. We are not having an experience of reality; reality is experience, and part of that is the experience of being a self that sees itself as a thing having an experience.

Reality is an ocean of experience, part of which is the experience of being a separate thing that is experiencing reality. If you contemplate this deeply, something begins to happen. You begin to fold in on yourself. As you contemplate reality as pure experience, you see that the experience of contemplating is contemplating itself. Some part of the ocean of experience has gathered itself up into a self-reflective swirl that bends and twists awareness in on itself. It is like a mirror trick that creates a being of light that comes to believe that it exists independent from the light that forms it.

If we contemplate the nature of who we are deeply enough, we discover that we are the experience of contemplating ourselves. There is no independent self contemplating itself. There is just an experience of a self that experiences itself contemplating itself in a mental pirouette that resembles a dog chasing its tail. This contemplation contemplating contemplation will always be existentially unsatisfying to us until the moment our twirling drills a hole in the ground below us, and we fall through the floor of our being into a deeper reality.

It seems that I have managed to get way ahead of myself right here in the opening pages. That is because the contemplation of reality and the possibility of liberating ourselves into a different one is so inspiring. I have had the privilege of falling through many floors of assumption about reality, and every one of them has opened into a journey of mystery and awe. The avenues for investigation and the conclusions that are presented in this book have come from my own experiences of spiritual revelation and my efforts to understand and articulate them.

Before we get too far ahead of ourselves, let's return to my opening statement which claims that the soul of a new self is forming in consciousness. This language is borrowed from the writings of the French paleontologist and evolutionary pioneer Pierre Teilhard de Chardin. Teilhard called the process at the heart of evolution "creative union." He saw the entire universe as conscious. Every part of the universe—atoms, molecules, organisms, planets, suns—is permeated by and inseparable from consciousness in unique ways.

According to the theory of creative union, evolution proceeds through the successive appearance of new conscious entities, which means it occurs as new selves are born. The first stirring of a new self is the appearance of a characteristic energy. This energy resonates in such a way that it attracts some of the separate elements at one level of reality into a new whole self at the next level. Atoms are attracted together to form molecules; molecules become cells; and cells become organisms.

When biological evolution reached a certain point, the process of evolution shifted its weight to consciousness. This shift was not simply the next step in the chain of being; it was a leap into a new level of evolution altogether. Evolution moved from the biosphere to what Teilhard famously called the noosphere—the layer of consciousness that surrounds our planet. The evolution of consciousness necessitates less biological change because a lot of change can happen in consciousness within our existing biology.

Those of us who feel drawn to come together to participate in the evolution of consciousness are being gathered by the attractive energy that is calling elements together that will ultimately form a new self. We are being pulled into the energetic eddy of an emerging self. I want to be careful not to be too literal about all this. I urge you to hold it all metaphorically—feel the energy and direction of the metaphor more than the meaning of the words.

Imagine a universe still and empty. Suddenly an attractive energy emerges—an invisible whirlpool appears. Elements that are attuned to that swirl of energy begin to resonate with its frequency and are carried toward the source of it. They begin to orbit around a mysterious center point, coming ever closer to each other. The pieces adjust to one another, finding ways to orbit more tightly with less friction and bumping. As this dance of unification reaches a critical level of density and speed, something happens. A burst of energy reconfigures and reconstitutes these elements into a new self. This new self sees from a vantage point that had never been available before. A new platform for perception is born, and the emergence of this new perspective immediately begins to refashion everything.

This is the process that we are being called to. We do not participate in evolution the way we participate in other endeavors. Evolution is not an activity that we do. We participate by making ourselves available to a process of self-creation that is already underway.

If this sounds far out and fantastic, I urge you to hold it all loosely, more like poetry than prose, and give me the space of this brief book to make it clear. In the pages ahead I will share what I have come to believe about what a new human could be and how we can participate in the journey toward it. This is primarily a book about inner transformation, but, as we will explore throughout, the distinction between the inner world of thought and feeling, and the outer world of body and action is ultimately a matter of convenience and not a real division anyway.

This is a good moment to insert an important inquiry that is foundational to everything else that we will discuss. We have already said that our customary perception tells us that we live in a world made up of separate things. We have been trained to see reality as a collection of objects. Hence we use the word *everything* to signify the totality of what is. This view of a world made up of separate things is built right into the structure of language. We have learned about different categories of things. There are physical objects like trees and automobiles, mental objects like memories and ideas, and social objects like marriages and countries.

The brilliant twentieth-century anthropologist and philosopher Gregory Bateson taught that all of the lines that divide the seemingly separate objects of our world are merely lines of human convenience. Have you ever been in a conversation when you realized that you were making a distinction because it was helpful to your purposes even though you knew it wasn't ultimately real? We often do this when trying to generalize people into categories. We say there are X kind of people and Y kind of people, but we feel compelled to add that we know that no one is either all X or all Y. We are making a distinction because it is helpful for the point we want to convey, and we feel compelled to acknowledge that it is not ultimately a real line of division.

Bateson was simply saying that all of the lines that divide things in the world are lines created for human convenience. They are not ultimately real lines of division, but for some reason or other it is useful to think in those terms. In truth, beneath all of these imagined divisions, everything is connected, and even more, everything is part of one continuous whole. Bateson believed that all of the major problems in the world are the result of the difference between the way we think and the way the world works—which means the separations we assume to exist and the reality of continuity. As long as we think in terms of a world of separation, we will constantly be acting in ways that oppose the true continuity that sustains existence.

When we treat an ecosystem as a collection of parts, we find ourselves destroying elements of it without realizing that in doing so we are damaging the whole. It would be like thinking that a finger is separate from the body and then cutting it off without anticipating the dramatic effect that action will have on the whole body, not to mention the person whose body it is. The challenge we face as a civilization is that we have been operating with a consciousness designed to understand by chopping reality up into identifiable pieces when in fact we live in a reality that is one continuous whole. It is critical at this point in our history that we embrace a new way of thinking that fully embraces wholeness and continuity.

There is one assumed separation that is most central to the discussion we are having right now, namely, the separation between you and the world. We have all been deeply conditioned to believe that we are separate entities, individual beings responding to different names and living independent lives. We assume that we are limited by our birthday on one side and the moment of death on the other. Between these two points we live "our life" as the person who we think we are.

If we look closely at the start of this imagined separate existence, we quickly find that designating the day we emerge from inside our mother's womb as the start of our existence is not truly defensible. Hardly anyone would argue that you didn't exist the moment before you emerged from the womb. If they did, they would first have to define exactly when you emerged from the womb. Was it when the crown of your head became visible? Maybe it was when more than fifty percent of your body mass was exposed to the outside? Perhaps the cutting of the umbilical cord is the magic moment when you separated from your mother?

We can take another angle and assume that it is the moment of conception when you came into being. Some imagine a moment during the development of the fetus when the soul enters the body. The closer you look, the clearer it becomes that there is no clear line of division that separates you from anything else. And yet we all feel deeply as if we are separate individuals, and we seem to experience uniqueness in ways that seem impossible to deny. This sense of separation is the topic of this book. How does it form? How is it maintained? And most important, how can we live beyond it?

Together we will be explorers in search of a perspective that will reveal our continuous, whole, and undivided nature. The best place to start this exploration is by looking into our understanding of mind. The commonly accepted view of the mind is that each of us has one. That view has become an assumption, at least in modern Western culture, that is seldom questioned. We can talk about "my mind" all day long and no one will ever object. And our experience seems to confirm the independence of our mind at every turn.

My mind is filled with my thoughts, not yours. I have my memories and not yours. When my finger gets pricked, it is me that winces in pain, not you. If we look at our experience, it is obvious that my mind is separate from yours. My feelings belong to me, and my memories are mine as well. One of the things that this book questions deeply is the nature of our experience. Does our mind produce experience passively, the way a mirror reflects whatever is in front of it, or is the mind creative and experience more like a story?

One of the most important questions we can ask ourselves is, how much do our beliefs about reality shape our perception of it? Our senses reach out and touch the world, and we imagine that we are seeing things the way they actually are. Most of us are aware that our perception of reality is imperfect. We see things as they are presented to us through a filter of ideas and presumptions. Even knowing this we generally relate to our experience as if it were a precise picture of reality. We respond to reality as it is presented to us with confidence and certainty. If we realize that we were mistaken, we can always make up for it later. Only in situations when the stakes are particularly high do we slow down and consider everything carefully. If we endeavor to participate in the delicate process of conscious evolution, the stakes are already high.

As I have been saying, our experience seems to continually prove and support our belief that we are separate from each other and have individual minds. Many of the world's great spiritual realizers and mystics would tell us differently. Their revelations of truth tell them that we are all one, that there is no gap between us. My deepest experiences of spiritual awakening have led me to the same unshakable conviction. Although we seem to exist as independent entities, one look beneath the surface of reality reveals that this is not the case. Beneath the veneer of conventional accepted wisdom we discover that we are all one. We look for the gap that would create the separation we feel, and we can't find it. If we look long enough or see deeply enough, eventually we realize that there is no separation.

Our experience is deeply embedded in the division between matter and spirit. We have an outer experience of matter that consists of all of the things in the world and our own physical form. We also have an inner experience of mind made up of all of our thoughts, ideas, and memories. Since at least the time of French philosopher René Descartes, we in the West have drawn a sharp line of convenience between mind and matter. We usually feel justified in holding onto such an assumption of separation, but we seldom ask ourselves on what basis or on whose authority we accept it. Why do we believe that mind is separate from matter?

At the turn of the last century, the American philosopher William James proposed a theory of reality that could resolve the split between mind and matter. He proposed a world made of pure experience. All that we have is our experience. I experience the cold smooth surface of the table in front of me. I experience thoughts and feelings arising in my mind. I experience my body, and I experience myself. Each of these is an experience. The difference between our inner experiences of mind and our outer experiences of the world is simply a difference in quality. Some experiences feel like they are of something outside, and others feel like they are happening inside of us.

Outer experiences are more permanent and persistent, and inner experiences are more ephemeral and fleeting. Our external experiences seem to connect to each other in certain ways. Our inner experiences also appear to connect in other ways. And finally our inner and outer experiences connect in yet a different way. External experiences have qualities, and inner experiences have qualities. The inner world of mind and the outer world are not two different realms of reality. They are simply two different qualitative categories of experience. Making a distinction between mind and matter based on qualitative differences has been very valuable for many reasons, and at the same time it seems that now a great deal of our global challenges stem directly from this misrepresentation of reality.

You experience a mountain in the distance, and you experience the idea that what you are seeing is a mountain, and you experience memories associated with this particular mountain. It is all experience. For convenience' sake we call some of these outer experiences of the world, and others we call inner experiences of mind. Regardless of what we call them, they are all experiences. The only thing we have access to is experience. Experience is all there is and all we have to work with.

The eighteenth-century Scottish philosopher David Hume had this same realization. He concluded that the only thing we have access to is experience and we have no way of knowing if our experience has any connection whatsoever to anything ultimately real beyond it. This insight left him peering over the edge of a cliff that threatens to fall into the nihilistic conclusion that there is nothing real at all. Rather than tread any further down that rabbit hole, Hume is reported to have spent the waning years of his life playing backgammon in public parks.

Later, existentialist philosophers like Friedrich Nietzsche and Jean-Paul Sartre dove head first over the cliff and embraced the inherent uncertainty of reality. They didn't necessarily embrace nihilism, but they did discover a profound capacity for creativity. Human beings have the capacity to recreate themselves. We can consciously choose to be a new kind of human. Embracing this level of creativity comes at a high price. We have to let go of the security of the known and embrace the unknown and the unknowable.

Existential philosophy invites relativism, which is the belief that all truth is relative and none of it is eternal or universal. Truth is always relative to some circumstance and set of conditions. Some facts are easy to see as relative. I see a large building across the street as I write, but it is only large as compared to the buildings around it. If I compare it to a skyscraper downtown, it is actually quite small. Other facts are harder to see as relative, and the idea that all truth is relative is one that many of us will resist because we feel that it leads to nihilism or the belief that there is no ultimate meaning in the world.

We are deeply conditioned to believe that the basis of truth is universality and eternity. We assume that facts that apply everywhere and always are more true than facts that are only true in some places at some times. When we consider that there may be no truth that applies always and everywhere, many of us feel uneasy. That seems to imply that nothing is true. Oftentimes we relate to relativism as if it necessarily implies nihilism. I don't believe it has to, and I believe that it is a risk we have to take if we are going to venture out beyond the known.

The new world and the new being that we are moving toward is one of continuity and flow. It rests in the recognition that reality is not a collection of things—static objects that move through time. Instead we see that everything is part of one continuous flow. We are not things that exist in reality; we are a manifestation of the flow of reality. William James defined his vision of a universe of continuous flow by identifying experience as the one stuff from which the whole universe is created. We can use James's terminology as long as we understand the meaning of the word *experience* must be dramatically expanded beyond our current human experience. If not, then we reduce the whole universe to an artifact of human experience and ultimately to the nihilism that most of us want to resist. This book is dedicated to articulating a view of one continuous reality and exploring the kind of beings we must become in order to inhabit it.

My deepest visions of a new reality came first in spiritual openings that occurred in deep meditation. While following the impossibly simple instruction of total acceptance of the way things are, I have on numerous occasions slipped out of my current experience of reality into something completely different. Those experiences have left me with a deep conviction that there is a different reality waiting for us. It is our destiny and our future, and it will not arrive without our consciously collaborating to manifest it.

In meditation practice I adopt a position of perfect passivity, allowing all experience to simply arise and pass away as it will. As I become more and more still, I lose all sense of myself. There is only the arising and passing of experience, and one experience that arises and passes away is the sense of being me, but there is no me having that experience. It is simply another experience in consciousness.

I am just another piece of experience that arises in the field of awareness. My body, my mind, my history, my qualities, my faults are all experiences that arise and fall away. The sense that all of these things point toward a being that exists independent of them is itself a transient experience that occasionally arises and falls away. There is nothing that exists other than fleeting experiences that rise and pass away in an unending parade. Our experience of reality is created from mental fragments in the same way that a movie is created from a rapid succession of snapshots.

The moments spent in this free flow of consciousness unrestricted by an enduring sense of self are more liberating than can possibly be described. There is no independent existence, nothing that is separate from anything else. This is what in Eastern mystical traditions has been referred to as the play of consciousness. The parade of experiential snapshots creates the illusion of reality. It creates the world as we know it. In this world we feel like a thing—an entity that exists separate from other things. We feel that we are a special kind of thing because we are an independent source of consciousness. We have our own mind that perceives both the inner world and the outer world.

We begin meditation by adopting a stance of passive acceptance in relationship to all of the content of our mind. Eventually we see that our experience of reality is being generated from perceptual fragments that pass through awareness. We awaken to what Buddhists call emptiness and recognize that reality is nothing more than a collection of fleeting experiences. This revelation is profoundly liberating, while it can be deeply disturbing. I remember the first time I began to feel myself slip into this state of consciousness. It felt as if I were going to die, even though I knew that I was just sitting on a meditation cushion. I didn't die, of course, but I did slide out of my self-concept into pure conscious awareness.

The meditation experience doesn't end with the freedom found in the emptiness of passive acceptance. That is just the doorway that leads to something more. The first stage of meditation allows us to become deeply absorbed in the space between all thoughts and feelings. It liberates our consciousness from the dictates of our usual habits of mind. In that stillness we begin to become aware of subtle movements and energies that move us physically, emotionally, and spiritually along a path of transformation that we cannot understand.

At times I have spent hours in meditation feeling that my body was being reconfigured. Sometimes it can be painful and uncomfortable, other times blissful and ecstatic; either way I simply allow it to occur. The meditative stance of passive acceptance now takes on a different flavor. It becomes an active passivity. I am still allowing whatever wants to happen to occur without willful intervention, but I am also aware of actively making myself available to be moved by spirit. I am not leaning toward anything in particular. I am simply leaning into deeper availability to a process of spiritual growth.

It feels as if forces far beyond my understanding are supporting and guiding a delicate process of awakening that I feel in my heart, mind, body, and soul. At this point it no longer feels as if the awakening is happening to me. I am having a localized experience of an awakening process that is happening in reality itself. A great deal of this book will be dedicated to the possibility of collective awakening in which a number of people simultaneously open to this higher source of energy and intelligence. In collective awakenings the presence of something bigger than any individual becomes particularly obvious and undeniable, but even individual awakening experiences bring us into contact with something much bigger than any individual.

Seeing that we all exist inside a world created from fleeting fragments of experience takes our normal sense of reality away. Suddenly we are not sure what is real. This can be frightening from the point of view of our current sense of self because it offers only disillusionment of that self. Any attempt to embrace the truth of absolute continuity and flow from our currently solid and fixed sense of self leads to unease. We cannot fully embrace a new reality from our existing sense of self because that self has no place in the new reality. A new reality can only be embraced by a new sense of self. In these pages we will embark on an exploration of just what kind of self is capable of stabilizing and abiding in the reality that I like to call continuity-unfolding.

I am compelled to explore what I see as two different aspects of spiritual practice and conscious evolution. They represent two levels of surrender. The first surrender is attained through perfect passivity. It is the surrender of letting everything go. The second surrender is an active passivity that moves us toward greater availability to the energy and intelligence of the larger being that we already are.

In my earlier book *Radical Inclusivity* I wrote about Edwin Abbott's 1884 novella called *Flatland: A Romance of Many Dimensions* and the exploration of multi-dimensional reality that it contains. I want to use that same book again here to illuminate our path forward.

Flatland is a world that only exists in two dimensions. It is a flat plane like a table top with no height. In Flatland the only thing you can see are lines. The actual being in flatland might be a circle or a square, but inside of flatland you can only see their edges. In the story only the mysterious entity visiting from the world known as Spaceland can see the surface of the circle or square because the Spacelander exists in three dimensions, not two.

The important insight here is that as long as we stay inside our existing reality our perception will have less dimensionality than our being. There is always more to us than we can see! The square in Flatland can never see its own surface because to do that it would have to jump outside of the two-dimensional world that it exists in. The three-dimensional being (perhaps it is a cube) already exists outside of the plane of Flatland, so the cube can get up over the square and see its surface.

From within our world we may see beings that have more dimensionality than we do, but we will only see those aspects of them that exist in the dimensions available in our world. When the cube from Spaceland crosses the plane of Flatland, it doesn't appear as a cube. It appears as a line because lines are all you can see in Flatland. The cube could never explain what it looks like in three dimensions. That possibility lies outside of the Flatlanders' capacity to imagine. The cube can't even explain the existence of the Flatlanders' own surface—the idea of surface is not even imaginable in Flatland.

When a three-dimensional cube passes through Flatland, it simply appears as if by magic. One instant it is not there; the next it is. No entrance from anywhere. It simply appears out of nowhere because from the Flatland perspective nowhere is exactly where it came from. If this line that appears as if by magic then tries to explain itself, the Flatlanders simply have no idea what they are talking about; they can't imagine it.

All manifest beings exist within a limited dimensionality. Dimensions beyond those do not exist for them. This book introduces a reality that exists beyond our own current level of dimensionality. Generally it is not visible to us at all. Occasionally we get glimpses of it. These glimpses, as seen from the vantage point of the limited being that we are, feel unintelligible and mysterious because our powers of perception have less dimensionality than that reality has.

I call the consciousness that gives us access to this high-dimensional reality continuity-unfolding. A vision of continuously unfolding reality can appear to us, and has to me, in deep meditation and in collective spiritual dialogue practices. If these experiences remain anchored to our current sense of self; in other words if they are viewed from within our current limits of perceptual dimensionality, we can only see a thin slice of that bigger reality.

If we are able to leave our current sense of self behind and float off into another dimension, something even more amazing occurs. If we not only "see" higher dimensions from here but actually leave here behind and move into higher dimensions, we can experience this new reality in its fullness. When we are inside of it, having left our limited self far behind, that reality appears to us as totally intelligible. In fact, it makes more sense to us than anything else we have ever experienced, and we have no doubt about its existence.

Imagine a Flatland square that lets go so deeply of its sense of reality that its consciousness floats up out of its current plane of existence. All of a sudden the Flatlander is seeing the impossible—squares, triangles, and circles, not as lines, but as surfaces from above. From that point of view, the Flatlander is standing in nowhere seeing everything, which sounds like descriptions mystics use to explain their spiritual awakening experiences.

I believe this is a very useful way to understand our own mystical experiences. They are journeys to other dimensions that occur once we have let go of our current sense of self and reality. These experiences are profoundly intelligible and seem to make sense of everything. When, and if, we return from such a journey, we find that squeezing back into the limited dimensionality of this world is uncomfortable. We also discover that what was so clear and simple and true out there is mysterious when remembered from back here. Our mystical journeys beyond our current dimensionality are often impossible to communicate to anyone else, unless they have had a similar experience.

Of course I am making all of this sound horribly dualistic, as if there were a reality out there that is separate from a reality over here. This separation is a line of division that is useful in describing our mystical experiences because our minds are conditioned to see things dualistically in terms of separate objects, and this description fits comfortably into those patterns of thought. Ultimately, however, it is not true. There are not two realities; there is One. Reality is one continuous whole without breaks or gaps. That is the core insight that characterizes the reality that we are moving into and that I am calling continuity-unfolding.

In this first chapter we have explored how we come to have perceptual glimpses of a new reality. We live in a world of things-in-space and have glimpses of a new world of continuity-unfolding. These glimpses, which we often refer to as mystical experiences, come in weaker and stronger forms. The weaker forms are glimpses of a new reality as viewed through the perceptual limitations of our current sense of self. The stronger forms are journeys that we take in consciousness beyond our current sense of self directly into a new reality. The weaker forms leave us compelled to continue. The stronger forms leave us convinced. The weaker forms have the power to initiate a true spiritual search. The stronger forms have the power to end it.

In the remainder of this book we will expand our exploration of continuity-unfolding consciousness, and more importantly we will discuss the possibility of not just having perceptual access to a new reality, but actually creatively embracing a new sense of self that can abide there. We can glimpse a new reality from our current sense of self. We can learn to liberate our consciousness and journey beyond our current sense of self into a new reality. But even more significantly than both of those, we can let go of our current sense of self and embrace a new one that allows our awareness to stabilize in continuity-unfolding consciousness. In this book I intend to share with you everything I understand about how we can stabilize in a new reality.

My experience tells me that this is not a solo journey. The sense of self that we must embrace is collective, not individual. We will not become a new being on our own. We will become a new being together. I have experienced this shift into a collective self with others. It is a miracle. It is almost impossible to describe, and yet I feel compelled to do so. You are invited to a journey that takes us beyond our current sense of self, beyond the experience of no self, beyond even an individual transformation of self, into a sense of self that only emerges between us.

The first step on this journey was to introduce the multi-dimensional nature of reality. The next step will be to begin the exploration of what our "sense of self" is and what might replace it.

CHAPTER TWO

THE NON-LOCALITY OF SELF

The formative years of my spiritual life were primarily shaped by two lineages. The first was the Hindu enlightenment tradition known as Advaita Vedanta. The second involved the evolutionary spiritual philosophies of Sri Aurobindo and Teilhard de Chardin, and later American thinkers such as Ralph Waldo Emerson, Margaret Fuller, Charles Sanders Peirce, William James, John Dewey, and Jane Addams further shaped my understanding. These influences combine in a powerful way to create a model of spiritual evolution as the growth of one dynamic and conscious whole being that is the inspiration behind my entire life.

My initiation into Advaita Vedanta was almost exclusively experiential. I read very little of the literature associated with that path during the early years of my spiritual life. I knew of some of the great masters of that tradition, such as Ramana Maharshi and Sri Nisargadatta, but I did not study much of their teachings. My work in this path was guided by an American teacher named Andrew Cohen, whose teacher, H.W.L. Poonja, had experienced an awakening with the Indian sage Ramana Maharshi.

Long years of intensive and disciplined practice have blessed me with repeated experiences of the already-liberated nature of my true being. Over and over again I was thrust into the recognition that the source of my consciousness was a free-floating awareness and, in words made famous by Nisargadatta, "I am that."

Experiences of this type are often referred to as non-dual awakenings. During these extraordinary episodes you recognize that the true nature of reality is Oneness. Reality is not a collection of separate things; it is all a manifestation of one consciousness. When this realization of Oneness is brought into contact with the perspective of evolutionary spirituality, the combination leads to a realization that can be described as *evolutionary non-duality* or, as we have been calling it here, continuity-unfolding.

In the previous chapter I outlined the premise of this book in terms of the emergence of the soul of a new self. The view that we are exploring tells us that by liberating ourselves from the restricted perception of our current sense of self we slip beyond our current dimensionality into the fullness of who we are. At that point we become available to participate in a process of reconfiguration that will result in the formation of a new sense of self. This sense of self is not going to be another version of a thinking-thing self. It will be something completely different.

We typically think of human beings as things, thinking-things. We see ourselves as entities that are aware of our own existence and are able to perceive and think in order to make conscious decisions. It may be more useful to think of human beings as a way of being. As I watch people walking in and out of this coffee shop, what am I seeing? As each next person walks up to the counter, scans their inner experience and decides between coffee and tea, am I seeing the individual actions of isolated entities or unique manifestations of a way of being?

Typically I assume that I am seeing separate, isolated individuals making independent choices. If I sit here long enough, I can start to see something different. I start to see a way of being manifesting itself. I start to see a range of possibilities being expressed in unique ways by each seemingly individual entity. So where does the sense of self exist? Is it within the individual or between them? As part of our journey of discovery, we will see that what we call "human being" is better thought of as a way of being that lives in the space between us. The sense of self is the primary carrier of that way of being, but that sense of self does not exist within individuals, although it is replicated there. We all hold a copy of it. In truth it really exists in the relational space between us.

The way of being human has changed throughout history. New eras of history are built on a new sense of self that gives rise to a different range of possibilities. In the European Middle Ages we were the ignorant children of an all-knowing God. With the advent of the

Enlightenment we became thinking-things capable of rationality and understanding. The Enlightenment brought with it new potentials that simply did not exist in the Middle Ages. At the same time there were things possible in the Middle Ages that we lost access to in the Enlightenment. For instance, the English poet and theologian Samuel Taylor Coleridge feared that the Age of Reason would be the death of imagination, and he advocated for the practice of what he called the "willing suspension of disbelief." And the Danish philosopher Søren Kierkegaard argued passionately for the importance of being able to exercise faith along with rationality.

At its most foundational level, a culture is defined by a sense of self, and that sense of self exists within the culture, not just in individuals. Analogously, the dance does not exist only within individual dancers; it exists in the relationship between the dancers as well. Dr. Jeffrey Kripal of Rice University has devoted his life to studying mystical potentials. He points out that the different cultures that exist on this planet currently have different ranges of possibility. Each culture has access to certain mystical experiences and not others. Expanding the range of mystical access in our culture is a primary focus of this book, but for now what is most important is to realize that the most foundational level of cultural development occurs through shifts in the sense of self, and as the sense of self that we hold between us shifts, so too does the range of possibilities available to us.

The process of self-re-creation is a process of defocusing and refocusing. We first allow our current sense of self and our experience of reality to fall out of focus. Then we lean into a refocusing process that is not happening inside of us but between us. This refocusing process is the birthing process of the soul of a new self. It is happening in reality, not inside of us. Reality is moving to a new equilibrium. It is shifting its center of gravity. The new focal point that it comes to will be permeated with a new sense of self. If we let go of who we think we are and relax into the universal process from which we came, our energy and consciousness will be reconfigured into a new way of being.

In the remainder of this chapter, we will take a closer look at the defocusing process. We will explore how to let go of our current sense of self and our existing perception of reality so that we are available to participate in the universal process of self-re-creation. Many of my experiences of defocusing came through the practice of meditation, so we will start this inquiry there.

In deep meditation we encounter our own non-existence, or at least we discover that we are not who, or what, we thought we were. We see that our experience is made up of a never-ending parade of passing experiences. These experiences are all real experiences, but we have no way of knowing if they are real experiences of something real. It occurs to us that even if we were to find definitive proof of some independently existing reality, that proof would come in the form of another experience. There would be no way of knowing what truth that experience was pointing toward either.

As we stated already, the Scottish philosopher David Hume realized this a long time ago. One of the contemplations he was involved with was an inquiry as to how he could know for certain that he was not dreaming right now. How could he know that his current experience was not actually a dream? He concluded that there was no way to be certain. This could all be a dream. So he preferred to play backgammon in public squares rather than face the deep uncertainty that lies beyond the edge of what we think we know. Later we talk about the existentialist philosophers in the early twentieth century who embraced uncertainty with vim and vigor, but even before that the German philosopher Immanuel Kant was carving out a space for uncertainty in the human experience. In his masterwork *The Critique of Pure Reason* he uses the word *noumenon* to describe the real reality that lies beneath our phenomenal experience. We all have access to a filtered and interpreted perception of reality—phenomena. Real reality lies forever beyond our reach, but it does exist even if we can't touch it directly.

Kant's view of reality is more or less the one that most of us hold today. It splits reality up into three parts—the really real, our perception of it, and us. It represents a big step forward for humanity because it allows us to embrace different experiences of truth without giving up on truth altogether. A world where everyone believes they have infallible access to the only actual truth leads to big problems because we assume that anyone who asserts a different truth must be wrong or crazy, and definitely dangerous.

The realization that we are all holding a perceptual version of reality and not a direct knowing of truth introduced a healthy uncertainty into culture. Over the last few hundred years we began to learn, sometimes slowly and painfully, to tolerate views that are different from ours. And we continue to improve our capacity to look beyond differences in order to discover the deeper truths that unify us.

The literary movement known as Romanticism actively embraced the idea of multiple perspectives. The Romantics were in part reacting against what they saw as the limitations of the Enlightenment. One of those limitations was that for all of its magnificent advances the Enlightenment thinkers were still in some ways committed to a single view of truth. It was not the truth of any particular person. They no longer believed that a king or pope had special access to the really real, but they did believe that natural law told us what was unquestionably true. The Western Enlightenment was a triumph for rationality and was certainly more tolerant of difference than the church of the Middle Ages, but to the Romantics it was still closed to the full immensity and mystery of life.

The novel *Frankenstein* by Mary Shelley is a great Romantic story that metaphorically teaches us about what happens when human beings think they can know everything. Life is bigger than we can conceive of. If we make the mistake of believing that we can understand and control it, the results will be . . . well, monstrous. Timothy Morton, also of Rice University, tells us that we are still in the Romantic era, and I couldn't agree more. Those of us whose imaginations have been captivated by the immensity of that which lies beyond our ability to grasp are captivated by the Romantic impulse. Poets and playwrights like Coleridge, Wordsworth, Shelley, Fichte, Goethe, Emerson, Longfellow, and many others wanted to expand our conception of reality. If the perspective shared in this book compels you, it is safe to assume that in your own way you are also a Romantic.

An astounding implication of Romanticism is that reality, at least as we perceive it, is in part created by us.

We are both a part of reality and a source of it. This was a very strange idea in the seventeenth century. The Romantics played with the creative and multidimensional character of reality by making cameo appearances in their plays. In a cameo appearance the author of the play plays a character in the story, effectively becoming the creator and a part of the creation at the same time. As you can see, the Romantics were trippy; in fact we will see later how they used mind-altering drugs to conduct experiments in consciousness.

For the Romantics our experience of consciousness was not something to be taken for granted. Our minds were not just mirroring reality back to us passively. Our minds were shaping our perception of reality. This is the insight that lies at the very core of so much of what we have come to call personal transformation. If our minds shape our experience of reality, we should be able to change our experience of reality by altering our minds. Reality is not something fixed that we exist in and have to take as it is given to us. Reality can be altered, and we can have a creative role in the creation of a new future. This insight, which is a very Romantic one, is the heart and soul of conscious evolution.

I see this book as a product and an extension of the Romantic imperative. Our spiritual awakenings and realizations confront us with an experience of a reality that lies beyond our current perception. When I have opened to experiences of emptiness, unconditional love, kundalini awakening, constant consciousness, divine revelation, and a host of other excursions beyond the known, the one thing that I was always left with was knowing that reality, whatever it is, is much bigger than I had previously thought.

Powerful awakening experiences can tempt us to move from one fixed view of reality to another. They tempt us to conclude that before we were not seeing clearly and now we are. If we stop there, if we pause at the very next step of the journey and claim it to be the truth, we miss a great opportunity. That opportunity is the direct realization that reality is so enormous and magnificent that there is always going to be more of it out beyond our imagination.

To me this is a huge relief. I don't want to live in a reality that is limited by my imagination. I want to live in a reality that will always be bigger than I can imagine. I want to live in a universe of mystery and enchantment. I will always keep striving to experience more of what is real, even though I know that beyond that there will always be more discoveries to be made. Falling in love with the opportunity for eternal discovery is very Romantic.

In a paradoxical way, the realization that the movement toward deeper truth is unending is an end to seeking. Our spiritual search begins with the conviction that there is something we are not in touch with that we want to find. Our things-in-space consciousness assumes that we are seeking for something specific—an idea, an experience, a realization—something that once found will end our search. What we find instead is that the search for truth will never end in any single insight or ultimate experience.

Our seeking for an endpoint comes to an end when we realize that there is no end to be found. What we finish with is the desire to possess an ultimate and conclusive truth. Our desire to come to the end of seeking is what comes to an end. At this point our spirit and our natural curiosity are free of any sense that something is wrong, even in the midst of perpetual uncertainty. The fact that there is always and forever more to discover is not a problem. It is simply the truth. Not knowing becomes more comfortable and more desirable than certainty because not knowing is exactly the state of availability and receptivity that makes all things possible.

I feel the need to remind you that I am writing this book in a Romantic spirit. My intention is to share conclusions that I have come to—my next steps on the journey. It is not meant to be final or definitive. It only explores one possible vision of a new reality. It is the one that I have committed my life to, and it may open your heart and mind as well. Embrace the ideas that I am sharing, but don't adopt them. Play with them. Think about them. Explore them. Allow them to take you somewhere you've never been before. Please don't read this book like an instruction manual or a scientific report. Read it like poetry. Ultimately all writing is poetry because it is metaphorical. It points toward a possibility that exists beyond the page and the words. As you read, allow your attention to wander toward a possibility that could never be captured in words.

We are charting a course to a new reality, and the glimpses we get of that are often seen through mystical insights and spiritual openings. Some of those openings come in the form of experiences of emptiness, and those experiences leave us with an obvious question to answer. As you begin to see through the illusion of self and sink more and more deeply into the consciousness between all thoughts and feelings, you see through the self. You realize that reality as you have always seen it has been constructed from fleeting experiences. You also realize that you are nothing more than a collection of experiences that appear to be associated with you. You can feel the conviction that you exist. You can feel assertions about this thought or that feeling being "yours," but you cannot find the actual entity that is supposed to be you. All you can find is yet another experience that seems to be pointing at you. When you look to see yourself, there is nothing there. The question you are left with is, who is seeing all this? Who are you?

If you find the courage to let the layers of identification fall away, you start to feel unhinged. You don't know who you are. The process of mind that creates the illusion of self becomes more and more clear to you. You see how feelings arise followed by assertions of ownership. "I feel like this." "This is my feeling." You see memories and images arising in mind all accompanied by the belief that they refer to you. When you look for yourself, you only find more thoughts, feelings, images, and memories that you assume are about you, but you never directly encounter yourself.

Eventually the thoughts, feelings, images, memories, and associations all start to slow down. They fall away, receding into the background of awareness. It is like floating on your back in the middle of the ocean. You can only see the sky above.

You can even go so far that you lose all sense of your body and mind. There is just seeing. This is often called the witness state. Who is this witness? Who is it that sees through your eyes and hears through your ears? What is the source of awareness, and where does it abide? The interruption of our self-concept does not extinguish awareness. The person who we thought was aware is no longer there, but awareness remains. Who is aware? What is aware?

There are many books that describe the source of awareness. Mystical traditions East and West have given dramatic testimony to the ultimate source of awareness. It is often thought to be the consciousness of the universe itself or God in her many forms. In the following quotation the Christian mystic St. Augustine describes his discovery of the ultimate source of awareness:

> My mind withdrew its thoughts from experience, extracting itself from the contradictory throng of sensuous images, that it might find out what that light was wherein it was bathed. . . . And thus, with the flash of one hurried glance, it attained to the vision of That Which Is.

The Hindu mystic Nisargadatta Maharaj, as I alluded to earlier, points to the awareness behind awareness and declares, "I am that." The following passage taken from his famous masterwork called *I Am That* describes the mystery of witness consciousness:

> I find that somehow, by shifting the focus of attention, I become the very thing I look at, and experience the kind of consciousness it has; I become the inner witness of the thing.

Finally there is the famous passage from Meister Eckhart:

> The eye through which I see God is the same eye through which God sees me.

Some mystical traditions have felt compelled to hold this experience of absolute awareness to be the ultimate goal of the spiritual path. Once we have transcended any limitations on our awareness, we merge with the ultimate source of all awareness. We realize for ourselves that there has always only ever been one consciousness behind all awareness. Freed once and for all from the illusion of separation, we abide in a state of blissful unity with all that is. We are the all-seeing eye of the world. Some traditions assert that our entire universe is held together by the consciousness of just a handful of individuals who have attained this level of universal clarity. Sufis and Sikhs have held for centuries that there must always be at least a few perfectly empty beings on the planet to act as channels for divine grace, and one of my favorite spiritual passages comes from the Christian mystic Thomas Merton, who makes a similar claim:

> I wonder if there are twenty men alive in the world now who see things as they really are. That would mean that there were twenty men who were free, who were not dominated or even influenced by any attachment to any created thing or to their own selves or to any gift of God, even to the highest, the most supernaturally pure of His graces. I don't believe that there are twenty such men alive in the world. But there must be one or two. They are the ones who are holding everything together and keeping the universe from falling apart.

Our normal perception of reality is so profoundly limited that even a brief glimpse of universal illumination leads us to the conclusion that nothing could be more important. After having lived an entire life inside an utterly convincing illusion of separation, even a moment spent in Oneness leaves us with a view so vast that words cannot describe its majesty. That is why spiritual wisdom has often been equated with the discovery of a pearl beyond price.

I once had the luxurious opportunity to meditate from morning to night for sixty days. At the time I was working with the American spiritual teacher that I mentioned earlier. What was particularly unique about the design of this retreat was that there was no stated endpoint. For all I knew I was going to be on retreat for the rest of my life. In fact as the length of the retreat expanded beyond one month I left my career as a schoolteacher in order to continue. The unspecified endpoint, coupled with my determination to see the retreat through to the end, created conditions that led to a profound cascade of awakening experiences that I chronicled in a book called *The Miracle of Meditation*.

At one point during the middle of that retreat I was in such a state of spiritual abandon that I looked up at the sky and cried with the realization that I really had no idea what lay beyond it. Somehow in that moment the sky had become a metaphor for the edge of human perception, and I was awestruck by how vast reality actually was. As the days of the retreat passed, I found that every next day was a new adventure. Each evening before falling asleep I would marvel at how much deeper and more full my experience was today than yesterday. I could feel myself merging with the mystery of reality more and more, and I began to hope that I really would be on retreat for the rest of my life. I was experiencing complete contentment, needing nothing, wanting nothing, and having no idea who or what I was. Life was a never-ending revelation flowing forever forward. My sense of self was just a part of this flow, not a separate being experiencing the flow from outside.

Experiences of this depth allow us to experience reality at its naked core. It is vast, alive, awake, and fluid. It contains no separation. Everything exists in a unified flow of incomprehensible being that has no edges and no gaps. This recognition of pure being has the power to liberate us from reality as we know it and from the sense of self that is so often left unquestioned. Suddenly we know that we are not an entity, a thing that exists as an isolated part of the universe. The universe has no parts. It is whole and undivided. The self is not separate from reality, witnessing it from the outside. The self and reality are one. The sense of self and the reality that it sees are one.

This is the ultimate return home. We have been away on a trip far from where we started without knowing it. We have visited a mysterious land full of isolation and division, and now we have returned home to the truth of Oneness and Unity. It is little wonder that for thousands of years many have held this spiritual homecoming as the end of the spiritual path.

There are other traditions, ancient and contemporary, that hold to a different view. These traditions see us not on a journey back home, but on a journey forward into the future. If the journey we are on is not only back to the beginning but also into the future, then the dissolution of our current experience of reality provides the opportunity to enter into a grand creative endeavor. Once we are free of the hypnotic trance of our current reality, we are available to consciously participate in the creation of a new way to be human.

These traditions are often inspired by a vision of universal evolution and recognize that our sense of self is an inseparable part of a larger evolving whole. Evolutionary mystics such as Sri Aurobindo and Teilhard de Chardin believed that our liberation as individuals was the first step in a process of conscious evolution. Only when we have become free of our current sense of self can we begin to participate in the creation of a new one.

The idea of conscious evolution gets truly exciting when we understand that the self is not just an image of ourselves that we hold in the privacy of our individual minds. The sense of self permeates reality like a scent permeates the air. You cannot separate the self from reality as a whole. Our current reality is inseparably linked to our current self. Reality is built by the sense of self, and the sense of self is created by the reality from which it arose. A new sense of self gives rise to an entirely new reality. And a new reality can only arise on the back of a new self. The self is both the seer and the reality that it sees. A new sense of self can only arise with the arising of a new reality, and a new reality can only arise simultaneously with the arising of a new sense of self. They are not separate. They are one.

Struggling to comprehend the complete non-separation of self and reality is a critical inquiry for those who want to fully understand what conscious evolution is all about. Those of us who have experienced the dissolution of self to any degree have likely already seen that as the self disappears so does the world. If later we return back to our self, as most of us do, the world comes back with it.

What if we don't return to the same self? If upon our return the self we emerge back into is different than the one we left behind, we will have been transformed and the world will have transformed with us. We do not return back to the old world as our previous self, and we don't arrive as a new self in the old world. We return as a new being in a new world. The sense of self cannot change without changing the world. Self and world are not two.

Our conditioning around being separate from the world is so deep that it is almost impossible not to see ourselves as a thing that exists in the world. Look around you now. I am still in the coffee shop filled with people. I experience myself as being over here sitting at this table, drinking this cup of coffee, and typing on this computer. I experience other people as being out there at their own tables or standing at the counter drinking their coffee. Because I see through these eyes, taste in this mouth, and pick up the cup with this hand, I call them my eyes, my mouth, and my hand. Over and over again I claim ownership of the things that I think belong to me—my body, my friends, my job, my wife. Who is it that the pronoun "my" refers to? I assume it is me. I assume that when I say something is mine that it belongs to an entity that is me. Yet when I look for that entity, I don't find it.

When I need to talk about myself, I use the pronoun "I" to refer to what I imagine to be myself. When other people want to refer to me, they use my name. Other people also talk about my body, my friends, my job, and my wife. Who is it they think they are referring to? The existence of the self is an assumption. That assumption is reinforced over and over again through my own constant assertions of ownership and through the continual affirmation of that ownership from others. The sense of self is not just an image of myself that exists in my mind. It is an assumption of self that exists in the constant affirmations in my own mind and in the minds of others and in my interactions with them. If the separate sense of self lives anywhere, it lives in this inner dialogue in my head and the outer dialogue in society.

The separate self, having been established and agreed upon, enters into a dance of constant affirmation. Having solidified the assumption of selfhood, the whole world becomes a symphony of confirmation. I decided to pick up the cup, and low and behold, it is in my hand. I walk down the street, and every passing building confirms that I am there. I only see the inside of this coffee shop. I can't see inside the shop across the street, of course, because I am over here. The fact that I see only this coffee shop and these people confirms my separate existence. Clearly I am here and not there.

Every moment my experience of the world offers generous confirmation of my separate existence. Every time I can only see through these eyes, taste in this mouth, or think with my mind, I am more fully assured that I exist as a separate entity. And yet we have said that our phenomenal world is created out of our sense of self. If I believe that I am a self that is restricted by a separate existence, then I will create a world that reinforces that belief. It is a self-fulfilling prophecy. What my current sense of self believes is possible becomes possible; what it believes is impossible remains so.

Our deep experiences of unity beyond separation reveal the truth of unlimited possibility. Reality is not limited. It is not bound. The sense of self shapes reality by filtering out of a field of unlimited potential only those experiences that fit within a preexisting framework of what is possible. Everything else remains unknown to us. The sense of self is inseparable from our phenomenal experience of the world. The self is created within a limited range of possibility and then filters out any information that might reveal more. What would happen if all of a sudden something changed? What if suddenly I could see out of your eyes or see the thoughts in your mind? Then my fundamental sense of self would have to be called into question. Luckily these things don't happen—at least not very often.

Immanuel Kant injected the beautifully awkward phrase "transcendental unity of apperception" into Western philosophy to explain how our perceptual world is created. The phrase, as clumsy as it may feel, is worth examining. Kant explains that we live inside a unified picture of reality because our minds filter and shape the enormous amount of sense data available to us moment to moment into a cohesive, if incomplete, picture of reality. This unified picture of reality, which includes world and self, is necessary for us to be able to function. If we were not able to filter and shape our perceptual picture of reality, we would find ourselves hopelessly lost in a chaotic avalanche of raw sensation.

The unified whole picture of reality is transcendent because it exists before everything else. It is our background conception of reality, a presumptive framework against which the actual experience of every moment is judged, valued, sorted, and molded. To say that unified picture is aperceptual simply means we can't see it. All of this judging, valuing, sorting, and molding is happening unconsciously. All we see is the final result. We just see the world as it is presented to us by the mind. In our ignorance we assume that the world is as it appears to us because we are unaware of how much processing has already gone into creating it. Our conviction in our own existence as a separate entity is constantly being affirmed and reaffirmed by ourselves, by others, and by the world. So it appears as if it must be true unless we realize that we are not seeing all the evidence.

The examination, evaporation, and transformation of our sense of self is the mechanism that allows us to play an active part in the greatest creative endeavor imaginable—the evolution of phenomenal reality altogether. Kant set the stage for the Romantic revolution and the birth of a mandate for participatory cosmic creativity. In the late eighteenth and early nineteenth centuries, a call to become a creator of reality began to burn in the hearts and minds of poets, playwrights, musicians, and philosophers who realized that they had a part to play in the growth of the universe.

What Kant called the transcendental unity of apperception in more modern terms has been called a worldview or a paradigm. The paradigm that we live inside of dictates the range of what is possible. It tells us what is real and what is not, and it controls our access to the tools of inquiry. We don't bother inquiring about the reality of unicorns because we already know they don't exist. Only when we liberate ourselves from our existing paradigm are we free to envision something truly new and different.

It is popularly held by many today that a shift in paradigm is imminent and that it will bring about a different sense of self and a new world. My contention in this book is that one of the most profound ways that we can participate in the creation of a new world is by liberating ourselves from our current sense of self and then coming together with others in a new one. This is not a process of construction. You can't build a sense of self like you build a house. It is a process of growth. The growth of a new self happens naturally, like a plant in a garden, as long as we create the right conditions for growth. This book is dedicated to creating the right inner conditions for the emergence of a new self.

In order to prepare ourselves for this magnificent creative endeavor, we must be willing to travel far beyond everything we know. The emergence of a new self and a new world is a wholesale shift in reality. We must let go completely of everything so that we are available to participate in the greatest opportunity the universe has to offer—the evolution of reality. One of the most powerful places to begin this journey is with a deep examination of our sense of self and the willingness to imagine a different one.

How can one sense of self envision its own replacement?

For twenty years I lived inside of an experimental spiritual community that was focused on the emergence of a new sense of self. The new sense of self that we ultimately experienced was a collective self. It was a self that exists between us, not in us. It comes into existence when individuals come together and give themselves to the extraordinary possibility of giving birth to a new way of being human. That experiment eventually came to an end, but the vision of us coming together in a new human possibility will never leave me.

We have been trained to assume that we are a separate self and that our sense of self is something we hold inside of us. In reality, the sense of self was never just held inside of us. It also lives in other people's perception of us and in cultural views about what it means to be human. The self that we are exists in all of us. It exists between us. It exists in the fabric of our interactions and relationships. We never were isolated individuals. Who we are was always contained in the whole. It lived out there in the matrix of relatedness that binds us in a way of being. At the most fundamental level, there is one self and we are it.

Deep mystical experience opens us into a non-dual view of reality where there could never be a sense of self that existed in one place separate from another. The sense of self would have to exist always and everywhere. Our things-in-space view of the world rests on a pervasive assumption of duality, and so we assume that our self is a thing that exists here and not there, now and not then. It is a sense of self trapped in an imagined state of isolation from the rest of reality. In fact the sense of self is not an object that exists in some specific place; it is more like a flavor in a soup or the sound of one instrument in a symphony. Where does the flavor exist within the soup? You can taste the flavor, but it is an inextricable part of the whole soup. The flavor does not exist in one corner of the pot; it is distributed throughout the soup. The sound of the instrument is spread across the symphony. Our sense of self is distributed throughout society and the world like a note in a symphony of being.

A deep inquiry into the nature of evolution gives us another access point to the direct experience of non-duality. What thrilled and terrified Darwin was not the idea that each species evolves into the next. The truth that he discovered is that when you look closely enough you find that there is no line that divides one species from another. What we had assumed was a collection of separate species, each independently created by God, are in fact all part of an evolving continuum.

The simple activity of walking gives us another angle from which to explore evolutionary non-duality. We assume that walking is a skill that humans learn and master, but another equally valid way to look at it is that walking is a skill that evolved out of this planet. Walking is not just something humans do; it is an orchestrated movement that happens in relationship between a human and the world. Walking is a dance in which we use our legs and feet and the force of gravity to propel us forward. It is a controlled fall. Walking is something that happens in the relationship between the planet and us. A deep contemplation of the evolutionary process ultimately reveals that everything happens in relationship. Nothing happens in isolation because everything exists as part of a single continuous whole universe.

As the journey of this book continues, we explore more and more deeply the non-dual perspective as it is experienced in mystical revelation and as it is revealed in contemplating the evolutionary process. As we continue, please remember to hold these words poetically. They are not labels telling you what is. They are not signposts pointing the way to truth. They are gestures, sweeping at times, that imply a mood and a direction. Like all forms of poetry, there is room for ambiguity in what is written.

The meaning you find has to be your own. To quote the great American Romantic Ralph Waldo Emerson:

> *Truly speaking, it is not instruction, but provocation, that I can receive from another soul.*

Our intuitions are experiences of a new reality come firsthand through the source of being. They cannot be captured in words and passed on as knowledge in their entirety because they can only be known through direct connection. Allow this book to provoke intuitive wisdom. Be open to the possibility of being transported into a direct encounter with a new reality that we can only enter together in a celebration of collective being and shared selfhood.

CHAPTER THREE

THE IMPLICATIONS OF BEING A BEING

Spiritual practices like meditation direct us to turn awareness back in on its own source. They are designed to bring us into a direct encounter with our own self. As I have already stated exhaustively, what we discover when we try to locate our self is that there's nothing there. Our experience is made up of a never-ending parade of snapshots of experience. This cascade of experience generates a sense of self that upon closer inspection does not exist.

There is no self. We had always assumed that our awareness was anchored to something, but in the experience of emptiness we see that there is nothing there. Awareness is. That is all. There is no one that sees, no one that hears, no one that thinks or feels in the way we had thought. There is just seeing, hearing, thinking, and feeling as experiences in the universal soup of being. These experiential snapshots are flavors in the soup, notes in the symphony.

What is a self? Is it just nothing, or is it a different kind of something than we had imagined? This, it turns out, is a very important question for moral and ethical reasons, as well as ontological ones. The quest to understand the self has captured the imaginations of people throughout time, and in our own age self-inquiry has become commonplace like never before in human history.

In this chapter we begin a contemplation of the nature of the self that will continue throughout the book. Let's start with the wisdom of the cognitive scientist Douglas Hofstadter, who claims that the self is a complete illusion:

> We create an image of who we are inside our self. The image then becomes very deeply entrenched, and it becomes the thing that we attribute responsibility to—we say "I", "I" did this because "I" wanted to, because "I" am a good person or because "I" am a bad person. The loop is the fact that we represent our selves, our desires, hopes, dreads and dreams: it is the way in which we conceive of ourselves, rather than the way we conceive of Mount Everest or of a tree. And I say it exists entirely in the loop: the self is an hallucination hallucinated by an hallucination.

The Danish philosopher Søren Kierkegaard some centuries earlier had expressed something similar using language that uniquely captures the mind-bending effect of the contemplation of self upon self:

> *The self is a relation which relates itself to its own self, or it is that in the relation that the relation relates itself to its own self; the self is not the relation but that the relation relates itself to its own self.*

Both Hofstadter and Kierkegaard are asserting that a self is a relation, or a relation of relations—a loop as Hofstadter puts it. It is a relationship that connects certain aspects of experience to other aspects of experience and then to an idea of a self that we assume lies at the center of it all. It is a set of relations that defines an "I" that we assume we are. All of reality is made up of experiences in relationship with each other. And the relationships that connect the experiences are also experiences of relationship. As the American philosopher William James put it, pure experience is the "stuff" out of which all of reality is made.

If a self is not a thing, what is it? The contemplation that we have embarked upon is a dizzying affair. In effect an assumption of self is questioning the assumption that it is. As long as we are identified with the assumption of self, this inquiry will keep pulling the rug out from under us. In order to even start to get some traction in this investigation, we have to find a new place to stand. I suggest that we stand in the assumption that a self is not a thing, but rather it is an arrangement of experience.

If we use the analogy of a river, we can say that the river represents the stream of experience that makes up reality. A twig floating in the river represents the self as we have imagined it. The twig is the assumed thing-self. The new self is not a thing. It is not separate from the river of experience. It is an inseparable part of the river. It is more like an eddy—a swirling current of water that spirals for a time on the surface of the river and then disappears.

If you see a swirling eddy on a river, it looks like something. You can see it; you can identify its borders, but try to pick it up, and you see it disappears. This is a pretty good analogy for the sense of self. It is not a thing that you can touch and separate from the whole. In the midst of the current of consciousness it appears to exist. But it is made of the consciousness in which it is recognized. If you try to see it in isolation, it is gone.

Think about this little experiment. Go up to a very still lake. Put a stick in the water and swirl it in circles until you create a whirlpool. Take your stick out of the water and watch the whirlpool. It will twirl for a time and then fade out and disappear back into the still surface of the lake. What a beautiful metaphor for a sense of self. Some energy starts a swirl in consciousness. That swirl becomes a self. This is akin to the loop that Douglas Hofstadter speaks of. The swirling self lives for a time and eventually returns into the body of water from which it was born.

We come to our spiritual practice convinced that the swirl of self is who we are. We sit in meditation, and we allow the swirl of self to calm until there is nothing left but the still surface of the ocean of consciousness. The self is gone, and yet awareness is still there. Who is aware if not the self?

One conclusion that we can draw from this kind of experience is that the ultimate source of awareness is the ocean of consciousness itself. The ocean is alive, and its awareness is what got swirled into a sense of self. In that swirl some portion of the ocean of consciousness concluded that it was a self and forgot the wholeness that it really was. In the deep stillness of mind that we experience in meditation we come home to who we are as the conscious awareness of the whole of reality. Spiritual paths that make this assumption are called paths of transcendence if their final goal is to escape the illusion of the separation and remain rooted to the realization of unity.

The challenge that this view can pose is that it cannot help but diminish the separate sense of self by limiting it to nothing more than a perceptual illusion. The self that we were, and that others may still believe themselves to be, is an untruth. This conclusion denigrates the separate self and devalues it to the point that it may lead those who follow such a path to ignore their own needs or the needs of others. There can be, and often is, something noble in self-sacrifice, but I have also seen unnecessary suffering justified with noble ideals. This leaves me compelled to examine any expectations of selflessness on the spiritual path very closely. The denial of the needs of the separate self does not necessarily reflect higher wisdom and can lead to harm of others or ourselves.

We are talking about a moral problem that is a challenge of idealistic philosophies. The attitude of idealism tends to promote the value of ideals over the good of individuals. This is seen dramatically in the lives that have been lost in wars over what may be very noble ideals. Clearly a case can be made for the importance of self-sacrifice and the ideals upon which sacrifice is made. There are many instances throughout history of unequivocally beneficial idealism. For instance, few would claim that the willingness to sacrifice for the cause of civil rights in mid-twentieth-century America was anything but noble. I am only cautioning that our zeal for a better world must be accompanied by a deep and abiding care for the people of the world.

The exploration that we have embarked on—to embrace the future of being human—has inherent moral implications because a new reality is a little like the Wild West. A system of values will not be waiting there for us. It is us who will need to decide what gets valued, what deserves our care and compassion, and what are just things that we can use for our own ends. If our experiences of transcendence lead us to the conclusion that the absolute awareness of the whole universe is all that really matters, inevitably the separate sense of self will be denigrated. It will be seen as less important or even worse as an obstacle to be eliminated.

One way for us to approach this important philosophical contemplation is to ask the question, What counts as a being? I believe this simple question is the most important philosophical question of our time. A thing is an object. It doesn't count as a being. We use things, manipulate them and subjugate them to our will. If I thrust a shovel into the dirt to dig a ditch, no one will ever report me for being abusive to the shovel. It is just a thing. Beings are allowed to use things for their own purposes. Beings are not allowed to use other beings, except within mutually agreed upon terms.

Beings are different from things. Beings have rights. As we speak about the future of being human, one of the things we have to address is the need to extend our current understanding of being. In our present discussion we are talking about extending selfhood to things that were not considered beings before. This means extending care and compassion to more of the universe. As the things of this universe are replaced by beings, there is more that deserves to be cared for. Things have no value in and of themselves. Their value is based on utility. If you can do something with it, it is valuable. If it is useless, it has no value. Beings are selves; they have inherent worth. How we decide what counts as a being dictates what is treated as intrinsically valuable and what isn't. That is why the question, What counts as a being? is the most important philosophical question of our time.

We are searching for a spiritual view that embraces the reality of both the universal self and the separate self. Both need to be seen as real beings with inherent value and worth. This means that both need to be seen as equally real. We are embarking upon this journey at an interesting moment in history because our species just went through a radical process that led to our separation from the world. During the fifteenth and sixteenth centuries, the Western world underwent a massive cultural upheaval often called the scientific revolution, the Age of Reason, or simply the Enlightenment. One way to understand that leap in consciousness is as a triumph of objectivity. This was a time when "objective truth" became king, and under its reign humanity enjoyed enormously positive material, social, and personal benefits. At the same time all of the gifts of the Enlightenment came with a cost, as a subtle, initially almost imperceptible, level of devaluation of our selves began to grow. To see how that problem persists into the present day all we have to do is look at the way that we are taught to think about how we think.

We have all been indoctrinated into what is called a representational model of mind. Think about comic-strip thought bubbles. How many times as a child did you see comics where something that was pictured in the outside world was also depicted inside a thought bubble that pointed to someone's head? The message we receive through this simple image is that our mind, presumably contained in our brain, contains representations of whatever exists in the world outside. We see by taking in information from the world and projecting it on the screen of the mind's eye.

This representational model of mind might be, and probably is, the source of many of the existential feelings of separation, isolation, and alienation that are so common in our world. When we talk about objective reality, what we commonly mean is that which is real even if we are not around. Objective reality—or the real world—is real, independent of us. The world is one thing, and it has its own reality, and we are a different thing with our own reality. We assume that if we are not seeing reality clearly it is because there are errors in our perception. To get to what is truly real we have to strip away any errors in perception or biases of judgment that we are holding. Reality, we imagine, is what is left when we are not adding anything to the picture. To get from our interpreted picture of reality to an accurate picture of reality all we need to do is get out of the way.

This all seems obvious to us; after all we are products of the modern age that was born out of the Enlightenment. We don't have a problem with the idea that we find out what is real by stripping away our false perceptions and biases. In some sense then we have been taught to see ourselves as the source of a deviation from reality, and so we strip ourselves out of the picture to find out what is real. Are we then unreal? Are we outside of reality looking in?

This kind of contemplation sounds nonsensical as long as it is happening within our things-in-space assumptions. The bedrock assumption of things-in-space consciousness is the assumption of infinite, three-dimensional space filled with things. Within our existing framework, the questions that we are asking cannot be asked because they call into question the framework itself. It is like pulling up the floorboards that you are standing on. You just can't do it. In the same way that person cannot pull up the floorboards under their own feet, a sense of self cannot question the self that is asking the question. To ask these kinds of questions authentically we have to slip out of our current dimensionality into the invisible fullness of our being. Only from that no-place can we truly engage in a contemplation of this depth.

The logic is not complicated; if reality is continuous, then we could not possibly be separate from it. But recognizing the truth of the logic is not the same as directly experiencing the truth of it. Returning to our metaphor of a river, we have already seen that our self is not something like a twig floating along separate from the river and made of a substance that is inherently different from the river. Our self is more like an eddy that appears as a swirl on the surface of the river. It is born, lives for a time, and then passes away. Just like we do. It is not separate from the river from which it came; it is made out of the same stuff—water—as the river is.

As I have already said, in deep meditation the swirl that is our self becomes so still that all that remains is the river of life from which it was born. That, some would say, is the end of the spiritual path. Others, as I have already said, conclude something different. They see this spiritual homecoming as the first step in a new journey. Once liberated from the swirl of self, whether through a spiritual practice like meditation or through some other means, we have the opportunity to participate in the most exciting creative endeavor imaginable—the birth of a new self.

Our experience is so deeply rooted in the sense of being separate from the world that it can be difficult to even begin to let in the implications of what we are talking about. Reality is not an expanse of empty space filled with things made of different substances. Reality is one continuous flow that appears to us now as a multitude of objects. We see many, but reality is one. This is poetically beautiful, and it aligns with the wisdom of the world's great mystical traditions. We can easily believe it, but do we experience it? Can we let the truth of this fact in so deeply that it transforms our being and reconfigures reality? That is the adventure we are on— the simultaneous transformation of our being and reconfiguration of reality. To accomplish this we must disrupt our habitual way of thinking and being, and embrace a vastly different possibility.

I have very often paraphrased Gregory Bateson when he says:

The major problems in the world are the result of the difference between the way nature works and the way we think.

This is why the endeavor of self-re-creation has inherent ethical implications. If the way we think is the cause of the major problems in the world, then there is a real demand on us to change the way we think. Here we are envisioning a resolution to this predicament that takes place in one great shift in our way of thinking/being—a sweeping movement from the consciousness of things-in-space to continuity-unfolding. In this gloriously reconfiguring leap of faith and imagination, everything, including us, is reborn anew. And as I have already stated, this is not something we can do alone. This rebirth of the human self and the reality that supports it is something we must discover together.

An inquiry into the nature of being and self requires a great deal from us. Being and self are as close to us as anything could be. They are the paradigm we exist inside of. If our investigation remains superficial, then it will tend to only involve variations of our current understanding of being. So when we think about the possibility of a new being or an extension of being we will tend to look for some new thing to call a being. This has already been happening. At one time in some places only white male landowners were considered beings. Everyone else was the property or slave of a white male landowner. Eventually we granted the status of being a being with inherent worth and civil rights to more and more people. Now in most places in the west at least legally every person has been granted the status of being.

Today there is a battle being waged about other members of the animal kingdom. Are they just animals, living things, without inherent value? Can we slaughter them to make pocketbooks out of? How about for food? Extending being in this way to more and more individual organisms is important and has obvious ethical implications, yet it is still happening within our existing paradigm. The extension of being that we need to consider must go beyond individual organisms. Can an ecosystem be given the status of being a being? How about a planet? Gaia is the name used to describe the world we live in as a living being, not just a dead planet with life on it. It takes a much greater stretch of imagination to attribute selfhood to a planet, but that might be exactly what we need to do. We have given corporations the status of being a being so it seems like we should be able to extend the definition to things like whales and the Earth itself.

Our investigation needs to go even beyond the attribution of selfhood to the planet because a planet, although not an organism, is still a thing. What is the meaning of being a being, or being a self, in a world without separation, where individual things are no longer being separated apart as the fundamental building blocks of reality?

To take this inquiry further it can be useful to switch the question we ask from "What counts as a being?" to "Who is the doer, and what counts as an agent of action?" An agent is a thing that uses its will to make conscious choices. We have been trained to assume that agents are always individuals or collections of individuals. The contention of this book is that our conceptions of being, self, and agency need to expand beyond the individual. The philosophical contemplation that we have embarked upon takes us far into uncharted territory. To borrow an example that I originally heard from Timothy Morton, we usually think that when I pick up a glass of wine I am the agent of action. I am the one who wanted some wine and decided to pick up the wine glass to drink from. Morton asks us to think about the possibility that the wine glass is the agent of action: that it calls out to us and beckons us to drink from it. We were attracted to the wine glass because the wine glass was attracting us. A door invites us to walk through, a chair to sit down.

As a teenager one of my favorite rock bands was the Talking Heads. In fact one of the most exciting concerts I ever attended was seeing the Talking Heads perform at a small arena called the Cape Cod Coliseum during their *Stop Making Sense* tour. It was magnificent. Their final rendition of "Burning Down the House" threatened to shake the rafters loose. There wasn't a single person who wasn't jumping up and down.

The Talking Heads were a thoughtful band. Most of the original members had been students together at the prestigious and innovative Rhode Island School of Design. Although I was too young to ever see them when they were playing local gigs in Providence, they always held a certain hometown appeal for me. Recently the band's leader, David Byrne, published a book called *How Music Works*. The book begins with an argument about where music comes from that is a fantastic inquiry into the question of agency. Who or what creates music?

We assume that musicians create music, or at least groups of musicians. In his book Byrne surveys the music of different time periods and different geographical locations and presents a different point of view.

Yes, it is musicians who write music, play instruments, and sing songs, but it is not musicians alone that create music. The venues available to play music in and the technology available to create instruments also have a profound influence on the creation of music. Music is made to be listened to, and it has to be listened to somewhere. In Africa music was generally played in expansive outdoor spaces, and drums are one of the few instruments whose sound carries well out there. Pipe organs sound great in the cavernous cathedrals of the Middle Ages, and guitars sound great in the small rock clubs where the Talking Heads would play.

We would tend to simply say that the musicians were limited in the kind of music they could play, but they were still the ones creating the music. I want you to consider a different perspective. Maybe it is not the musicians who are playing the music. Maybe that is just the way we have been trained to think about it. What if the music were not coming out of the hearts and minds of the musicians alone? What if the music was emerging from the circumstances of the time and place where it would be played? What if music was not created by people but by circumstances and environments? Would that make the whole circumstance the agent, the being, the self?

Matthew Syed was a table tennis champion in England, and for those who might not know, that means being a major celebrity. Those of us in the United States may not pay much attention to table tennis, but that is not the case in England. Syed was a major public figure, which meant interviews and press conferences. Everywhere he went he was praised for his talent. Eventually he couldn't take it anymore, and he wrote a book called *Bounce* to bust the myth of talent.

We assume that winning a sports championship means something about the person who won. Mainly we assume that his or her victory was a product of talent and hard work. Sure, Matthew Syed had talent, and he worked hard, but those things alone were not responsible for his victory. Lots of people are talented and work hard, and the vast majority of them don't ever get the chance to participate in a championship match.

In his book Syed explains that he won a table-tennis championship because of circumstances that included his dad buying him a table-tennis table, the fact that he and his brother both loved playing for hours at a time, and that he happened to go to a school that had a fantastic table-tennis coach. Alter any one of those factors, or any one of dozens if not hundreds of other factors, and someone else would be the celebrity. Syed's argument is that it was not him as an individual who won the championship. The true victor was a complex set of circumstances and contingencies of which his talent and hard work were only a part. In the end he was the one who picked up the trophy and received the acclaim, but it was not he alone who was responsible for the victory.

The shift in perspective from individual agency to circumstantial agency is critical for those of us who endeavor to liberate ourselves from things-in-space consciousness and emerge into a universe of continuity-unfolding. I believe this is the direction we need to lean further into. We need to see that actions are not coming out of things but out of circumstances. You could call this an emergent perspective. Actions emerge out of environments, out of circumstances.

This is a wonderful contemplation. Think of anything that you currently think that you do and ask yourself who is really doing it. If you keep going, you will come across something interesting. Let's try it. In Syed's case he couldn't have won without his dad, his brother, and his coach. But he also needed his mother or he would never have been born. He needed a culture that developed and appreciated table tennis. He needed a planet that could evolve a species that could play table tennis, and he needed a universe within which planets that could support life evolved. How do we decide where to draw the line that separates the champion table-tennis player from the rest of the universe? It is very convenient, in the Batesonian sense, to draw a line around Matthew Syed and call him the victor, but the truth is much more complicated than that.

Let's look at another example, my writing this book. I am writing it for sure; at least it is my fingers that are punching the keys and my mind processing the thoughts and putting them into words. Where is all the information coming from? I would have to trace through more than half of my life and recount hundreds of relationships to be able to account for everything that is being shared in these pages. Am I the author, or does authorship have to be distributed among all of the individuals and circumstances that have made it possible for this book to be written?

Think of the last interesting conversation that you had. You probably assumed that you were the one who was producing the words that were coming out of your mouth, and of course the other person was producing the words coming out of their mouth. Would you have produced the same words if you had been talking to someone else or even to the same person under different circumstances? How much was that conversation a product of a whole set of circumstances? What credit do you really deserve?

One analogy that I am fond of using to illustrate this point is talking. When we talk, words come out of our mouths, but we don't say that our mouths are talking. We feel perfectly justified to claim that we are talking. Responsibility for talking is not given to the final organ that happens to vocalize the words. The whole being gets the credit. Even though I am the one who is sitting typing out this book, the real credit, on an existential level, has to go to a vast and complex array of circumstances. This book didn't emerge out of me. It emerged out of all of those circumstances. I am urging you to shift from a perspective of individual agency to one of circumstantial emergence. If you can make this transition, you will discover a new world where conversations, books, music, and champions emerge out of circumstances like flowers grow from a garden.

I certainly don't want to tip the scale in the other direction and diminish the central role of the musician, the athlete, or the conversationalist. Of course they were a critical part of what happened. Still, in our culture we have been trained to overemphasize the role of the individual almost to the exclusion of all other factors. This is going to need to change because it just isn't accurate. In a continuous universe you cannot single out any individual to receive credit because there are no individuals that can be separated out from a continuous whole. We have to begin to see circumstances, environments, histories, and contexts as doers. This means we have to begin to entertain the possibility of circumstances counting as beings. Can a circumstance be a self? In this book I am going to argue that it can, and ultimately I will illustrate that argument with a few experiences that were so dramatic that they have irrevocably altered the course of my life.

The great evolutionary mystic Pierre Teilhard de Chardin saw that a continuous reality required a new way to think about agency and began to think in terms of emergence. He looked at the history of our planet and saw a succession of spheres—spheres of possibility, you might call them. The geosphere was the domain of the nonliving material—the planet made of rock and water and air. The biosphere is the sphere of plant and animal life. And finally Teilhard saw the mental layer of our world, where the inner world of thoughts and feelings become possible, and called it the noosphere.

One hundred years prior to Teilhard the American poet and mystic Ralph Waldo Emerson expressed a similar understanding of the noosphere. In his essay called "The Poet" Emerson wrote:

> *The poet is the Namer, or Language-maker, naming things sometimes after their appearance, sometimes after their essence, and giving to every one its own name and not another's. . . . The poet names the thing because he sees it, or comes one step nearer to it than any other. This expression or naming is not art, but a second nature, grown out of the first, as a leaf out of a tree.*

Emerson did not see the origin of language as the individual mind. Like Teilhard, he also saw the mental activity of symbolic understanding as an outgrowth of the planet itself. Matthew Syed's championship grew out of circumstances, and so did David Byrne's music. Those circumstances emerged out of the noosphere, which emerged out of the biosphere, which emerged out of the geosphere, which emerged in the universe. From this ultimate viewpoint everything is emerging out of the universe as a whole. We have been taught to think of the universe as an inanimate place that is separate from us, but it is not. Our universe is a living being that has generated life and intelligence. Our universe is alive and whole. It is not a place. It is a being.

In our moments of deepest revelation we realize that we do not exist in the way that we had thought, and neither does anyone else. We have assumed that we were thinking-things that make independent, considered decisions. As we begin to suspect that this might not be true, we feel compelled to follow consciousness backward to its own source.

If we follow the trail of inner mysticism, unraveling the mysteries of consciousness, we will eventually discover a single, universal, and absolute source of consciousness. All is One. If we follow the path of evolutionary mysticism, we will discover that everything happens as part of a singular process of cosmic unfolding. Again, all is One.

The paths of mystical non-duality and evolutionary non-duality both lead to the realization of Oneness. Once we discover the singular Self Absolute in either its mystical or evolutionary form, we have to decide how we are going to relate to the relative self that we thought we were. How much do we, in our current form, matter? And how much responsibility do we have?

As we move beyond a consciousness of separation, we also move beyond easily identifiable beings, selves, and agents, and so we must consider the moral implications of how we define them. If we only see a self as a relation that relates itself to itself; if it is nothing more than a self-referencing loop that spins like a dog chasing its tail, is it a being that deserves to be cared for? Is it a self that can be held responsible for the consequences of its actions? If Matthew Syed did not really earn his trophy, should he get one? If he can reasonably deny responsibility for his championship victory, can a criminal similarly deny responsibility for his crimes?

We live in a cultural matrix that constantly reinforces a sense of independent and isolated existence. This is simply not the way it is. We are not entities that can be entirely separated from our surroundings. The discrepancy between how we think about ourselves and the way things are is the cause of many of the problems we see in the world.

When we see through the illusion of separation, it unhinges us from our current reality and opens the possibility of creating a new one. At the same time it also severs us from many of the cultural and ethical norms that guide social behavior and hold communities together. We find ourselves adrift, left to navigate the transition from this world to the next without clear guideposts. The ethics of separation are not sufficient to guide us into the reality of unity. We are between worlds without a map.

In this chapter we have been considering the fundamental questions concerning what is a self, what counts as a being, and who is the agent of action. These are inherently moral and ethical questions because what counts as a being is what deserves to be cared for. Only active agents can be held responsible, and it is unclear if what we currently consider our self is either a being or an agent.

Those of us who choose to pioneer a new way of being will need to be deeply engaged with questions of a new morality. To successfully navigate through this transitional phase between who we are and who we will be, we must accept responsibility for the consequences of our actions even while the nature of being, self, and agency remain unclear. We will not necessarily be supported by existing cultural norms on the open seas of a new way of being. We will have only each other to look to while we chart our course forward. We have lived in an ethical value system based on an assumption of individual agency, and together we will need to discover a new morality for circumstantial emergence. It is us who will figure out how to be in a new world.

CHAPTER FOUR

THE THINKING-THING SELF

Our minds function by taking in sensual information and then filtering and organizing that data in prescribed ways to produce a consistent experience of reality. Call it a paradigm, a worldview, or a transcendental unity of apperception—it all means that what we experience as real is an interpretation of reality. Our minds don't mirror reality to us; they shape it for us. During an episode of spiritual opening, we are temporarily liberated from the shaping of the mind. During these peak moments, to some degree or another we see reality uncensored. This can be an overwhelming experience that sometimes leads us to see through the illusion of separation and open into the Oneness of all that is. In these moments we realize that the separate being that we thought we were never existed independent of the All that we are.

If from this experience we conclude that we are home—that we have reached the ultimate truth—then we will rest. There is nothing left to do. If, on the other hand, we conclude that we are part of an evolutionary process, then we will be inspired to participate in the re-creation of a new sense of self. This is the conclusion that I have come to, and this book is about the new self that we have the opportunity to become together.

The process through which the mind shapes our experience is called conditioning. We are conditioned to see things this way and not that way. This conditioning is both personal and cultural. By personal I mean the shaping that has resulted from the experiences of this lifetime. The methods of traditional psychology have been developed to help us see through the negative aspects of our personal conditioning. We experienced certain traumas in our childhood, and those experiences shape how we see the world and other people now. At the level of personal experience, we are all so different. Things that I am afraid of you enjoy. I see things that you don't even notice. That person over there finds something easy to accomplish that you and I can't even imagine succeeding in.

The conditioning we inherited from culture is more deeply embedded in us than our personal conditioning. Family is a sphere of conditioning. My grandparents were born in Portugal and settled in America in a coastal city on the eastern seaboard. I have conditioning that comes from my family, and I see things and value things in ways that are similar to other second-generation Portuguese Americans. My family was also a particular family of unique individuals, and I share attitudes with my other family members that I do not share with other people, even other Portuguese Americans.

When I travel to Europe, the feeling of being American rises to the surface of awareness. When interacting with Europeans, I become so aware of my Americanness. I talk too loudly and directly. My perspective and opinions can be crass and cavalier. The value for my independence and freedom is paramount, as is my willingness to stand up for the rights and freedom of others. It isn't to say that only Americans have these characteristics, but in a very general way my travels abroad have brought me to become aware that there is an American character, and I have it. I am it.

If we embark on a journey beyond all conditioning, we find layer after layer of ideas and assumptions about what reality is and how everything works that are shaping all of our experience. At the bottom of this mountain of conditioning we find a fundamental experience of being human upon which everything else rests. This is the foundational assumption that all other assumptions assume. It is a set of ideas about what a human being is that all of our other experience is filtered through.

What we discover is that we live inside of a model of being human that shapes all of our perceptions and is the primary arbiter of what we see as real and what we determine is and is not possible for us. This model of being human is the most foundational source of our sense of self. From this starting point, layer upon layer of identity is built until at the top of it all I experience myself to be Jeff, a Portuguese American with a unique personal history, living out an individual life.

I believe that it is possible for us to experience beyond the foundational filter of being human and gain the freedom to re-create what it means to be human in the most profound way.

Our species is now a global force that shapes the environment of the planet and affects every living creature. We are limited by our sense of self, and our current sense of self seems to be reaching the end of its ability to successfully respond to the complexity of the world. We are seeing in many different ways our powerlessness to navigate effectively through the immense complexity of the world. Trying harder as we are will not be the solution. My firm conviction, and the contention of this book, is that the birth of a new self-sense is the key to our future.

Our planet and our future need us to come together in the most magnificent act of creation ever attempted—the conscious birth of a new self. The human self as it currently exists must give way; it must yield to a higher form of self. This birthing process must happen consciously. Another sense of self isn't going to be born and overpower us. We must participate in that birth. We must let go of the limits of separation so that a new form of self-conscious awareness can emerge between us. This book is my attempt to share everything I have experienced about how that miraculous act of creation can happen.

In this book you will find my attempt to articulate a completely different model for human being. When we use the phrase "human being," we most commonly mean a particular kind of entity. We think of a human being as a very special kind of organism. Special in large part because we have brains that seem to be able to think and feel in unique ways.

We all imagine that we are things that think. We see ourselves as having a body with a brain in it. There are five different senses that take in information about the world and feed it to the brain. The brain collects all of this incoming sense data and constructs our experience of reality, which is a more or less accurate reflection of the world outside.

This is what I call the thinking-thing self, and it is the most fundamental picture that each of us holds about who we are. At this point in human history, the thinking-thing self is pretty much the only option available to us for how to experience being human. We don't have another choice. You can't go to a psychologist and get a new experience of being human. You can get a better version of thinking-thing self, but you can't get something that is not a thinking-thing self.

For as long as we can remember we have lived inside this sense of self—this particular experience of being human. This sense of self is not the limit of who we are. It may be part of who we are—and even this is debatable—but it is definitely not the whole of who we are. The sense of self that you are living with has been constructed and refined for hundreds of years. You absorbed it wholesale from the culture you were born into without anyone even knowing that they were giving it to you. It is, in fact, only one possible way to experience being human. It is the source of everything that we currently know as the human world, but it is not the limit of what is possible. All of the tremendous wonders and achievements of human beings and all of our atrocities came from the gifts and the shortcomings of the thinking-thing self. Beyond this sense of self a whole new world is waiting to be born.

The first thing to grapple with in engaging with the ideas in this book is that our sense of self, the experience of being human that we are having right now, is not the only possibility for how we can experience ourselves. Take a moment to look at your experience right now and know that whatever it is, it is not the only option.

It takes a big shift in perspective to move into a different experience of being human. As I already said, you can't just get one from a psychologist. One of the places people have reliably gained access to alternative experiences of being human is through mind-altering drugs, and we can get some real insight about how we think about ourselves if we look at how we relate to these drugs.

Many individuals throughout history have used intoxicating substances to gain access to other experiences of self. The vast majority of those, at least in the Western world, do not relate to those experiences as equally legitimate options for being human, or even as signs that other possible experiences of self exist. Most people relate to their drug-induced experiences as illusions produced by electro-chemical distortions of brain function. This tells us a lot about how we understand ourselves.

If you were to tell someone that you had just taken LSD and were experiencing a different way to be human, they would probably remain calm and relatively unmoved. "Of course you are, you're tripping," they might say. What they are implying is that you are no longer in reality. You are on a trip away from reality, and therefore it is not alarming that you are experiencing something as impossible as a different way to be human.

I don't mention this to advocate drugs as a beneficial means to experience new realities—although there have been various movements and individuals who have. From the English romantic Thomas De Quincy to the psychedelic pioneer Timothy Leary there have been a string of respected artists and intellectuals who saw drug experiences as powerful access points to higher consciousness. I bring up the whole notion of drug-induced experiences only to use them to highlight some culturally held beliefs about reality that are illuminated when we look at the typical social response to drug-induced states.

As I said, the typical response to reports about drug-induced experiences is to assume that they are fantasies produced by aberrations in perception caused by altered brain function. It is assumed that the drugs disrupt your normal perceptual mechanism, so we experience a warped version of reality. The situation is analogous to looking in a funhouse mirror. You see yourself as impossibly tall and thin, or unbelievably short and fat. You don't think of these as alternative possibilities equal in validity to your current normal self. You recognize that they are perceptual distortions of reality caused by the curve of the mirror. They are not alternative realities.

The belief system in operation here is one that assumes that there is only one reality and that that reality is more or less the way we normally perceive it to be. In other words we see ourselves as beings that have a more or less accurate perception of a reality that exists outside of us. In this book we are saying that this experience of an outside reality that is viewed more or less accurately is a reality that is created by being a thinking-thing self. It is not the only possible reality; it is the one that a thinking-thing self such as me will see. This is another way to understand the loopy nature of the sense of self. The sense of self sees reality and creates it at the same time. How do you escape from such a trap?

The thinking-thing self is the one that we have all been acclimated to. It is the way we experience ourselves to be. It is what we believe a human being is, and if we have experiences to the contrary, we are much more likely to ignore or discard them than we are to take them seriously. Those few individuals who do take their alternative experiences of being human seriously often find themselves confused, alone, or both.

This book is also a message to all of you who have experienced alternate possibilities of being human and do take them seriously. You might be onto something important, and you are not alone.

It was René Descartes that first articulated the understanding of human beings as things that think. In the centuries since, we have become so deeply embedded in that experience of self that it is almost impossible to even consider another possibility.

There are two foundational assumptions that underlie the experience of the thinking-thing self. The first is that we are independent entities defined by the physical form of our bodies and existing in isolation and separation from all other beings and the rest of the world. The second is that we have a remarkable organ called a brain, which takes in sense impressions from the world outside and produces an experience of reality that is more or less accurate.

The thinking-thing self assumes that it is experiencing reality the way reality is. And one of the things that it experiences is its own self. We assume we are the self that we experience ourselves to be and that our experience of ourselves is more or less accurate. If we take drugs and experience some other possibility, we most likely assume that the drugs disrupted the brain's functioning and gave us a false image of ourselves. It may be fun for an afternoon, but it is not something to take seriously. It is something to recover from.

In my own life I never took my drug-induced experiences seriously because I knew that they were created from the drug and not a reflection of reality. Later when I had even more uncanny experiences in the spiritual practice of meditation I did take them seriously. I had only been sitting still, and slowly a completely different possibility for who I was opened up in my experience. There had been no mind-altering drugs, no incense, nothing. I was just sitting, and the whole world shifted and me with it. This wasn't a drug-induced state, and I couldn't doubt its reality.

The image of ourselves as a thinking-thing, a brain encased in a body, is the image that the inquiry of this book asks you to question. Are you really a thing that thinks? Does thinking happen in our brains? Is our physical body really the limit of our self? These questions and others will need to be examined if we want to explore what the future sense of self might be.

The way we relate to mind-altering drugs reveals something about how we understand the capacity for consciousness that we have. When chemicals affect our brain, we assume that what they are altering is brain activity. When brain activity is altered, our experience of consciousness is affected because we believe that consciousness happens in the brain.

A shaman would see things differently. Mind-altering substances are often used to induce shamanic journeys, but the shaman relates to his or her "trips" as real journeys, not as alterations of brain function. These journeys are actual movements from one place in consciousness to another. This illustrates one of the fundamental flips in consciousness that needs to occur in order for us to shed the skin of the thinking-thing self and enter into a new reality of consciousness unfolding. Consciousness is not something that happens in the brain. It is not something that we are producing, and it does not exist inside of us. Consciousness is what we live inside of like a fish lives in water or a bird flies through the sky. Of course not everyone would agree with this, and even those of us who do are often more anchored to our thinking-thing self-image than we imagine.

Some of the strongest opposition to the living-inside-of-consciousness view comes from recent discoveries in neuroscience that lead many to the conclusion that a lot of what we experience as real is only a creation of the way our brains function. Some such as the German philosopher Thomas Metzinger would even go so far as to say that our experience of reality is nothing more than an epiphenomenon of synaptic impulses. Everything you are experiencing right now is being created by the electrical discharges that are going off constantly in your brain, and we have no idea if that brain-induced experience has any relationship at all to anything we could call real. Maybe everything we are experiencing as real is no more real than the drug-induced delusions that we mentioned earlier. Your experience of being yourself reading this page right now might be nothing more than picture shows created from the electrical discharges in your brain.

Let's follow this particular point of view a little further down that road and say, as David Hume feared, that perhaps there is no reality at all. Maybe there is no space, no time, no things, no self . . . no anything. It is all an illusion created by the brain, a perfectly deceptive virtual reality. Although this idea can be helpful in unseating our fixation with reality as it is, and it is great fun for speculative fiction films like The Matrix, it is not a possibility that I feel particularly compelled by. That partly represents a commitment on my part to there being something real in reality. And it is also due to the fact that I believe the whole argument suffers from a fatal flaw of logic.

Let's imagine that it is true that everything that we are experiencing is an illusion of reality being created by our brains. That would mean that the brain itself is part of that illusion. All of the studies and experiments that were used to understand how the brain functions and to come to the conclusion that reality is an illusion produced by the brain are themselves also part of the illusion that the brain is creating. Can one part of the illusion be responsible for creating the rest of the illusion? If the brain is the thing producing the illusion of everything else, doesn't that make the brain real? And if it is, then doesn't the body that the brain exists in also have to be real? And if the body is real, isn't the world that the body emerged out of also real?

We can't believe that the reality we are experiencing is an illusion created by the brain without giving to the brain the great honor and privilege of being the only real thing in the universe. If we want to do this, we then have to find the line that separates the brain from the rest of unreality. Only then would it be reasonable to imagine that the brain was responsible for creating the illusion of everything else. In the example of the movie *The Matrix* that line comes in the form of there being two levels of reality. At one level Neo is a superhero, an awakened virtual being running around in a virtual reality. At another level he is strapped to a chair with his brain wired into the virtual reality of the Matrix. The seated Neo with the wire coming out of the back of his neck is the real Neo living in the real world. The virtual world of the Matrix is being generated from the real world.

Unfortunately, if we look closely at our own situation we don't see any hard dividing line. We don't see a real world that could be the source of our virtual reality, and if we did we would have to admit that the dividing line was also part of the virtual reality created by the brain.

The so-called "hard problem" of consciousness is figuring out how a grey mass of synaptic discharges leads to the rich and full phenomenal experience of reality that we have. This may not be the best question to ask because the brain itself, as well as the experience of being someone who has a brain and is thinking about the hard problem of consciousness, is already happening inside of the experience of reality that we believe is being created by the brain. Imagine a movie that is about a group of people who begin to suspect that they are not real people but are actually images being projected on a screen. Those familiar with Plato's cave analogy will see that some human mysteries haven't changed much in the past few thousand years.

Getting back to our movie of projected people who are beginning to wake up to their predicament, how can these people, who are images projected by a movie projector, ever hope to figure out how the movie projector that is creating them works?

I do believe that our experience of reality is being filtered and shaped. What we are seeing is an interpretation of reality, not an independently existing reality. In a sense then, yes, we could say that we are living in an illusion. I also believe that the illusion of reality that we are experiencing is connected to a larger, really real reality. That larger reality is the source of the illusion, and our spiritual-awakening experiences are glimpses into that higher reality. What we discover in our moments of illumination is that we exist in a reality much wider than we are capable of experiencing in our current mental configuration. There are dimensions of reality that already exist just beyond our reach.

There is another metaphor that can be useful here. Once again it involves a movie theater, and it has been employed many times as an analogy for spiritual awakening. In this analogy spiritual awakening is equated with realizing that you had thought that you were a character in a movie and then realized that you had actually been watching a movie while sitting in a theater the whole time. You had mistaken the story of the movie for the reality of who you were. You had identified with one of the characters of the film so deeply that you actually thought it was you.

The two uses of the movie theater analogy presented above illustrate a profound point that might be easy to miss if it is not pointed out. In the first instance the characters in a movie realize that they are actually projections on a screen. In the second a person in a theater realizes that he or she has mistakenly identified with a character on the screen. In the first instance the projection wakes up to the reality of being a projection. In the second a real person in the theater wakes up to the reality of who they always were.

This brings us back to the distinction we made in the first chapter. In the first instance a new dimension of reality is seen from inside of the existing available dimensionality. In this case the *character* on the screen is waking up to his or her predicament. In the second instance *we* are waking up to a new dimension of reality, in this case the reality of being the person who has been watching the film all along.

When we dare to inquire into the nature of our self, we inevitably encounter the loopy quality that Douglas Hofstadter described. In this analogy, for instance, what happens if the movie we are watching is about a person who realizes that they are watching a movie? How do you wake up from a dream that is about waking up from a dream?

I am not compelled by any line of inquiry that inevitably ends by making an illusion out of everything. I want to preserve the reality of brains, bodies, plants, planets, and stars. What I do want to question is the thing we call a self and particularly the thinking-thing experience of self that most of us are walking around with. I also want to inquire into how the thinking-thing self that we are is shaping and limiting our experience of reality. Investigating how my sense of self shapes my experience of reality is like picking yourself up by your own bootstraps. How can the self that is shaping reality look back on itself to understand how that shaping is taking place?

My contention is that we can't. In order to conduct an investigation into the nature of our self we must have a foothold in a dimension of reality beyond it. We cannot sail a boat unless our sail is in contact with the wind. We cannot drive a car unless its tires are in contact with the road. We cannot investigate our self unless we are connected to some reality beyond it. And I believe if you are reading this book you already do.

As we embark on this adventure, we must consider the fact that it inherently necessitates a certain level of disappearance. When we think of a new sense of self, we can't help but think of ourselves as someone who will have a new sense of self. But who is it that will have that new sense of self? A sense of self can't get a new sense of self. The new sense of self replaces the old one. The sense of self that thinks it will get a new sense of self will not be there when the new sense of self arrives. That is how far out we have to go. This is the most creative endeavor a human being can partake in. It is creativity at the level of the self and asks us to let go of who we think we are so that we can discover more of who we really are.

Another spiritual metaphor that is often used for awakening is the common experience of waking up from a dream. According to this metaphor, spiritual awakening means waking up from a dream. You thought that you were the dream person living your dream life, and then you woke up to find that you were actually in bed asleep the whole time.

Experiencing a new sense of self is similar. You are in one sense of self, and all of a sudden you wake up to a completely different sense of self. The important thing to keep in mind is that you are not the one who is going to wake up. You—the person you believe yourself to be while you are reading these words—are the dream self. The experience of being human that you are having right now is the one that is going to be woken up from. The interesting question here is, Who is it that will wake up?

As you will see, this book rests in the premise that a self-sense is not something that individuals have. It is an organizing principle in consciousness. A self-sense organizes perception, and one of the perceived things that it organizes is itself. The sense of self generates a particular picture of reality, and part of that picture is the experience of being someone with a sense of self that they live inside of. A self-sense is a characteristic of consciousness, not a characteristic of an individual, because the experience of being an individual is part of the self-sense.

Our current level of consciousness is powerful enough to hold a thinking-thing self and the world that a thinking-thing self generates. Self-aware beings in that consciousness necessarily experience themselves as thinking-things because that is the only sense of self that is available. If we give birth to a new sense of self, then that new self becomes available in consciousness.

It is tempting to say that this new sense of self will be available to us, but that is misleading because the "us" that it would be available to is the one being born. We are not going to develop a new sense of self. We are a sense of self that will participate in the creation of its own replacement. What will replace us? And what new and unimaginable capacities will that sense of self have access to? As the self-sense evolves in consciousness, new capacities of consciousness become available. This is the most creative endeavor we can embark upon, the surrendering of our current sense of self into the creation of a new one.

If we think about what it would mean for humanity to evolve to a new level of consciousness, the essential shift that would need to occur is a shift in the sense of self. What characterizes our current level of consciousness is a particular sense of self—a particular sense of being human.

It feels like something to be a self, and what it feels like is what needs to evolve. From one very powerful perspective we could say that the evolution of consciousness happens through the evolution of the sense of self. Consciousness evolves as the sense of self evolves. As the experience of being a self changes, new perceptions and new capacities become available. This is how consciousness evolves.

If we were able to have the experience of being a medieval serf in the eleventh century, I imagine we would hardly recognize ourselves. The experience of being human would be so different that it would feel completely alien. That sense of self was capable of holding only so much potential and possibility. There was a limit to what was possible in that configuration. It isn't that people were just not as intelligent. There were intelligent people—geniuses in fact—all through human history, but their genius was being filtered through a sense of self that was inherently limited in its perceptions and capacities.

You could not go back to the eleventh century and merely educate a person into becoming someone like you. If it were possible to facilitate a shift like that in an individual, it would have to come about as an entire shift in the sense of self. They would not only need more information and understanding; they would need to become a different kind of person. Their experience of being human would have to change at the most fundamental level. If we want to evolve consciousness, we must aspire to become a different kind of person— or, it might be more accurate to say, yield to the evolution of a different kind of person.

Most of us probably recognize the massive insufficiencies of the current level of human consciousness. We see unimaginably complex social, political, and ecological problems and the ineffectiveness of our current systems to address them. I could go on describing the challenges of our world, but there is probably no need to review the undeniable evidence pointing to the necessity of higher human consciousness.

Our sense of self and our ability to shift our experience of it sits at the center of the solution. Our current sense of self has reached the limits of its ability to effectively cope with the complexity of reality, and it needs to shift. What it needs to shift into is the subject of this book, and that discussion will continue in the chapters ahead. First, however, we need to outline a philosophical conception of mind that will help us expand the parameters of this inquiry from the outset.

I have already stated that I don't see that "theater of mind" theories of consciousness afford much support for our inquiry into the next sense of self. There are theories of mind and consciousness that I do think are valuable in this endeavor. These theories explain the brain not as a thinking-thing in the world but as an embedded part of a conscious system. The brain is an organ, and it does play a primary role in processing information, but it does so as part of a system, and whatever we call consciousness or mind is a function of the whole system, not just the brain.

What is the mind? Most of us think about it as a storehouse of ideas and memories. It is the place where we experience the world. Sometimes we might think about it as a movie screen that exists in our head and plays a continuous feature film with us in the starring role. Or we think of it as a computer that thinks and figures things out for us.

What is the relationship between the mind and the brain? If we don't think too deeply, we probably simply think that whatever the mind is, it happens inside the brain. We all know that the brain is the place where little electrical signals snap back and forth and that somehow all of those electrical impulses add up to our experience of the world—our thoughts, sensations, feelings, and memories.

The fact is that no one knows what relationship the spongy grey thing under our skull has to our experience of mind. It is a big question mark. People have theories, but no one knows for sure.

Recently, I read Alva Noë's book *Out of Our Heads* for the third time. The book starts with the assumption that the best way to understand the mind is to look at it functionally by asking the question, What does the mind do for us?

The mind allows us to interact with the world. Minds develop in relationship with the world, and they only exist in relationship to the world. Mind is not something that exists in the brain, although some brain function is certainly related to the mind. Mind exists partly in the brain, but also in the body, in our body's interaction with the world, and in the world itself. The human mind is an ongoing, self-organizing relationship of human beings and the world. Rather than thinking of the mind as a movie screen or a computer, Dr. Noë suggests that we should think of it as a dance.

If you go to a dance performance and the person next to you leaned over in the middle of it and asked, "Where is the dance?" you would probably look at him oddly. But the question is a good one. Where is the dance? The dance is not in the brains of the dancers, although the brains of the dancers are involved with the dance. The dance is also not in the bodies of the dancers, although the bodies are a crucial component of the dance. The dance exists in the relationship between all of the dancers and the stage and the costumes and the scenery. The dance is the whole ongoing interactivity of the event.

In the same way we should not look for the mind in the brain. The mind is the whole interactive event of human beings living in relationship with the world. The mind exists between all of us and between all of us and the world. The mind is not a thing; it is an interaction. Just like a dance is an interaction. The mind is a performance that includes events that happen in the brain but is not limited to them.

This theory of mind opens a doorway for us to begin to envision a new sense of self. Just as the mind does not exist in the brain, the sense of self does not exist inside of our bodies or our lifetimes. The idea that we are a self that is limited to the edges of our skin and the moments of our lives needs to be questioned. As we look more and more closely at the sense of self, we will see that it is not something that exists in us.

Like the mind, the self is something that exists between us. It lives in our interactions with each other and with the world.

The self is not a thing; it is a way of being. It is an organizer of human perception, behavior, and interaction. The thinking-thing self allows us to perceive reality in certain ways and not others. It allows us to act and interact in certain ways and not others. The sense of self places limits on the possibilities of being human. The particular set of limits dictated by the thinking-thing self has created tremendous advances in human life over the past few hundred years, as well as catastrophic failures. If we want to transform what is possible for human beings, we have to transform the sense of self. Consciousness will shift as the sense of self does.

The aim of this book is to introduce you to a new conception of selfhood. It is a self that is not fixed in a particular being. It is not limited by our habitual sense of separation. It is more of a dancing selfhood—a selfhood that does not exist in beings but between them. It is a collective self that is not the possession of any one individual. It belongs to many. I believe this is the sense of self that humanity is evolving toward, but before we can explore it more fully I want to spend a couple of chapters developing how our current sense of self emerged in the first place.

CHAPTER FIVE

COMMITTED TO BEING ME

In the last chapter we spoke about the most profoundly conditioned and deeply unconscious level of self-identity. At the very bottom of our experience of being human we experience ourselves to be a thinking-thing. Before I am Jeff, before I am a Portuguese American, even before I am a man, I am a thinking-thing. This is the bedrock of our current human experience, and it is exactly what the present inquiry has been designed to unseat, but before we continue with the dethroning of the thinking-thing there is a conversation that we need to introduce first.

We have been asserting that the sense of self appears in consciousness like an air bubble in water. The process of energetic coagulation that we have been describing is a universal process governed by laws and forces. If the sense of self were simply the natural outcome of a universal process, then there would be little else to say about it, but it is not only that. The self is also a self-aware platform for perception and a locus of choice. The self grows out of this universe like a leaf grows out of a tree, but it is a leaf that is aware of its own existence and has the capacity to exercise a limited amount of choice inside the universe that gave it birth.

We are talking about two different levels of being. At the universal level a process of creative union generates a new soul energy that gathers together the scattered parts of a new self into a harmoniously coherent being. At the individual level of being, a self-referencing loop in consciousness gains the sense of being a separate, unique entity.

This binary system yields our amazing potential for conscious evolution. When the loop-the-loop of self-referencing begins to become aware that it is part of a larger process, it simultaneously begins to feel compelled to play in that larger arena. No longer satisfied with the endless chasing after its own tail, this universally awakened sense of self can no longer be satisfied with life within the constraints of its current level of being. Knowing that there is more out there, it has a compulsion to escape from the limitations of separation and isolation.

I recently encountered the fascinating term "maze brightness" in the writings of a spiritual teacher named E. J. Gold. The term refers to a form of enlightenment that occurs in certain lab rats. Certain experiments conducted on rats involve having them hunt their way through mazes in search of cheese. Presumably by altering the maze and watching numerous trials you can glean some understanding of the level of intelligence the little animals possess. It seems that among a small percentage of rats something interesting happens in the midst of scurrying around in search of food. In a flash of insight they suddenly appear to realize that they are trapped. They instantaneously seem to become aware that there is more to the world than what they experience in the maze.

This leap of insight is called maze brightness, and once it occurs the rat is no longer interested in finding its way through the maze to the cheese. Now its only interest is in getting out of the maze altogether. What an interesting analogy to the situation of awakening to the loop of self-referencing. Once we realize that we are not really a separate individual but are in truth a little bit of consciousness that has been cut off from the rest through a maze of self-identification; once we have that flash of insight that tells us there is a whole world that exists outside of the boxes that we are trapped in, our interest in life within the boxes dulls. We can no longer be satisfied with life as it is, and we begin to search for a way out. For some of us that is how our spiritual search begins.

In my own case I seemed to come into this life with some degree of retained connection to the wider world beyond it. As a young child of three or four years old, I would periodically retreat into my parents' bathroom to access the wider reality beyond the world I had found myself in. The practice was simple. I locked the bathroom door and stared into my own eyes. As I looked into the eyes that were looking out at me, my being began to expand. I rose through the roof of the house, into the outer atmosphere of the Earth, and eventually to the limits of the universe. Having confirmed my connection to the reality beyond the limitations of the world, I would return once again to life as the little boy staring into his own eyes in the bathroom.

Perhaps the act of staring into my own eyes served to remind that little boy that he was really just a loop of self-referencing. From that recognition I seemed to gain the freedom to float beyond myself. My spiritual search began on the day that I lost access to this miraculous practice of expansion. In the years to come I experimented with self-created forms of meditation. At the age of about seven I would lock myself away, this time in my father's car, and in that cocooned silence search for a way to escape from the relentless stream of thought that I had concluded was separating me from the wider world beyond. I searched in vain for a crack between two successive thoughts that I could slip through.

From these early beginnings my spiritual life began. I had lost access to the wider life of the universe, and I knew that I was in a trap. As I grew toward adulthood, I found it difficult to be authentically interested in the world around me. No one was talking about how we were going to get out beyond this sense of being separate and isolated so that we could once again know ourselves to be universal beings. Since there was no one to talk about what really mattered to me, I began to forget about it. It was only much later that I began to have spiritual awakenings that opened me up once again to the universal nature of true being.

In our present discussion the form the maze takes is our current sense of thinking-thing self. We are trapped within the limitations of separate selfhood and expend much of our energy running around in an ever-shifting maze of limited possibility in search of the human equivalents of cheese. For different reasons and at different times some of us attain the maze brightness in the form of insight, revelation, and illumination.

So here we are reading this book, exploring the universal nature of our being and aspiring to create a new self in the universe. The maze brightness that has awakened our passion to live beyond our current sense of self is often attained through some fleeting experience of universal being. As we have discussed, one form of escape from the maze of separate being is to find a way to live from the universal nature of our being. This has been the path of great saints and sages of all ages. Their deep and continual abidance in the universal currents of reality have catalyzed the awakening of millions of others to the universal.

This book is mapping another route of escape. Not the transcendent escape into universal being, but the evolutionary escape into the next form of selfhood. Rather than leaving the process of becoming altogether, I advocate for a participatory process of reconfiguration into a form of self that we cannot imagine. It will involve a snake-like shedding of our current self-skin and rebirth into the next. And as we will see, we will need to climb into this new self together. It is not a new coat of identity that we wear as an individual. It is a new vessel of selfhood that we enter together heading toward a new future.

In order to participate in this collective reconfiguration we must understand the nature of our participation. How do we as self-referencing loops participate in the process of our own re-creation? To understand this we have to first understand how we are currently participating in the existence of the separate sense of self. Our sense of self is not something that exists independent of us. We are creating. We are participating in holding certain elements of reality close and pushing others away. This dance of pushing and pulling creates the sense of boundary between what we experience as our self and others. The remainder of this chapter will be devoted to one description of how this self-creating activity is currently being performed by each and every one of us.

You are not just a thinking-thing. You are a particular thinking-thing. You are an individual with a name and a unique character and history. You are a specific somebody, not just a generic one. In this chapter we want to examine how this sense of unique being is maintained within the undifferentiated sea of universal being.

I am about to take you into a wormhole inquiry. My earlier book *Radical Inclusivity* was entirely about the nature of wormhole inquiries, and I want to mention them again briefly here before we proceed. A wormhole inquiry is a philosophical investigation into some aspect of reality that has the power to shift your consciousness. A wormhole in space is a mysterious place where two universes touch. If you fall into a wormhole, you move from one universe to the next instantaneously. A wormhole inquiry is an investigation that holds your attention near the edge of a spiritual wormhole. By keeping your mind busy there you increase the chances of falling through into a new reality.

The art of wormhole inquiry is finding a way to come to rest in the delicate middle place where you are totally engaged with the inquiry at the same time that you avoid becoming overly involved with the content of it. You need to be locked in the investigation, sincerely attempting to find a solution, while at the same time being available for a nonlinear burst of insight in an unexpected direction. A wormhole inquiry is not designed to generate a solution. It is designed to increase the likelihood that you will fall into a different perception of reality altogether. Avoid getting too hung up on the arguments I am about to present. Hold them loosely and metaphorically. Follow the investigation wholeheartedly on its own terms and see what happens. Be more interested in where the inquiry is taking you than in what it is telling you.

Okay, here we go. At some point during our lifetime we became self-aware. We became aware of our "self." When we did, we discovered that we were somebody. We were a being, a specific person, a self. We had a name, and we were in the middle of a history that was unfolding. We were someone.

When we hear our name called, we turn. We assume this is because we recognize that someone else has called us. They shout out a name that we recognize is associated with us, and so we turn. We assume that we are a being that learned it has a name and then learned to turn when that name was called. That seems obvious, but it may not be accurate. In fact, it may be completely backwards.

We assume that we were someone first, and then we learned all kinds of things about who we were and how we should be. In this chapter we will challenge this notion, flip it around, and show that it might be more accurate to say that first there were a number of learned ways of being, and only later did we start to gather all of these into a sense of self. The sense of self came second, not first.

Our normal interpretation of why we turn when we hear our name called pivots on the assumption that we recognize ourselves to be a thing that can be labeled with a name. We assume that we respond to the call of our name because we recognize ourselves to be the person whose name is being called. We respond to our name because we know who we are and we know which name is associated with us. This seems so obvious that you might wonder why I keep repeating it. It is such a deep assumption that we can hardly see it as anything other than the truth of the way things are. That is why I keep repeating it, to be sure that you can recognize it as an assumption rather than just the truth of the way things are. This almost unquestionable assumption—that we are a something that is labeled with a name—is not a fact; it is an assumption well worth examining.

We think that responding to our name is something we choose to do, but how did the habit of turning when our name is called actually develop in the first place?

It probably happened because our mother, father, or other caretaker repeated our name to us over and over again at different times. One day we responded with a nod or a smile or a squirm. When we did, our caretaker responded back with delight and affection. At that point we had no understanding that what we were responding to was a name that referred to us. We didn't have any understanding that we were a thing that had a name. We happened to respond to a particular sound, got positive feedback for it, and eventually learned, or were conditioned, to always respond to our name. We started responding to the sound of our name long before we had any idea that it was a name that stood for us. We simply developed a habit of responding to that particular sound. We were beginning to be conditioned to experience ourselves as a particular and unique something that could be named.

Only later, once we had some mastery of language, did we learn that the sound that we always turn toward is actually a name that refers to us. The idea that I am a person who has a name came much later than the habit of turning toward the sound of the name.

"Oh, that sound that always makes my head turn towards it is my name. It is a label that refers to me. I am the person who has that name."

The significance of this is subtle but tremendously important. We were not "somebody" who learned to respond to his or her name. First there were interactions between human beings that led to the creation of a habit of responding to our name. Only later did we learn that we were a somebody with a name to respond to.

So what was it that was given a name? Was the name given to a being or to a set of habits? Is it the giving of a name, the labeling of a somebody, that turned a certain set of conditioned behaviors into the experience of being a somebody? Maybe we were not a somebody who learned to respond to a name. Maybe there was a habit of responding to a name that later learned to wrap itself up in a sense of being somebody. As our sense of self developed, the initial habit of responding to a name became a habit of assuming that we are the somebody who responds to that name. Over time we embrace more and more habits of being into an ever-expanding sense of self. Maybe selves are not things; maybe they are habits that are embraced as our self.

At different points during our very early lifetime we learned habits, like turning when we heard our name, that only later would be incorporated into a self-sense. These habits made us look, act, and feel like we had become aware of a "self" that had already been there and had now learned all of these new ways of being. We assumed that there had been a self there all along and that we were only now discovering it and learning what its name was. That isn't true. The self is a concept that we learn to wrap around a set of experiences that we relate to as belonging to the entity that we assume ourselves to be. There is no self that those experiences are pointing toward. They are just experiences labeled as mine, and there is an assumption that there is some "self" behind them all. We have been taught to imagine that at the core of our being there is a self, a somebody, that all of our experiences belong to. Maybe this is backwards. Maybe there is first a collection of experiences and only later do we draw a line around them and call them me.

Maybe we aren't born with a self. We learn one. A self is not something you discover; it is a habit, or a set of habits, that you learn. And like any habit you can learn new ones. In this book we are exploring the magnificent possibility of learning a new habit of selfhood. Before we start to talk about the new self, though, we have a little more to examine to understand how we learned to be the self that we already are and how we can break that habit.

Human beings are self-aware. We are able to perceive our "selves." How did we learn to be self-aware? When you look in a mirror, you know you are looking at yourself, but how do you know that? How did you come to understand and to recognize that there was such a thing as you that exists in something else called the world?

You learned to self-reflect in a two-stage process involving conversation. First you learned to speak out loud to other human beings, and then you learned to speak internally to yourself as if you were another. Thought is internal dialogue that you use to address yourself as if you were another person. This internal dialogue is the source of our self-awareness.

Before I go any further I want to be clear that I do not mean to imply that you don't exist except as self-talk. There is an important distinction between the "I" as subject and the "me" as object. The "I" is who I am. It is the being that sees through my eyes, feels through my heart, and hurts when I cry. The "I" is the completely mysterious subject of all of my experience. It is the mysterious part of myself that is the one that always sees, perceives, and feels but can never be seen, perceived, or felt.

Some traditions say that the "I" is one universal being that animates all of us. Others identify it as an individual soul that is the source of our particular and unique being. This is an important and fascinating discussion that we will return to later in this book. For now I simply want to make a distinction between the "I," whatever it is, and the "me" that is an objective sense of self that has become so deeply internalized that it has melded with our experience of ourselves. It is the "me" self that we are exploring in this chapter.

To make the distinction of "I" versus "me" clearer, notice that you can say, "I am going to the store," but you can't say, "Me am going to the store." In most forms of English you can say, "Take me to the store," but you can't say, "Take I to the store." That is because the pronoun "I" is refers to an active agent—"I"s do things. A "me," on the other hand, is an object that gets acted upon. An "I" is a someone; a "me" is a something. The "I" is the internal experience of being you, while the "me" is the external view that other people have of you and that you have of yourself. Using more technical terminology we would say that "I" refers to the subjective sense of self, while "me" refers to the objective sense of self.

This all seems simple and obvious enough until you ask the question, Where did the sense of "I" and the sense of "me" come from in the first place? And why are they split apart?

As a newborn baby you didn't have any ideas about yourself. But other people started to develop ideas about you. She is cute. She is good. She is fussy. She doesn't sleep well. And so on. The people around you started to form a "me" for you before you could even hold one in your mind. And they started to shape you into what they considered to be a more ideal form of "you" almost immediately.

As we already described, they did this by being sure to inject positive feelings into your nervous system to make you more likely to do the things they thought were good for you. Your loving caretakers repeated this conditioning over and over again, probably in the sincere hope that over time it would support you to become a "good" girl or boy, at least in their estimation.

As you grew older you acquired language skills. Of course by then you had already begun the process of becoming a "me" by being shaped into a certain set of behaviors by the responses you received from your caretakers before you could even speak. Once you were able to understand sentences you could really start to learn about the "me" that you had already started to become. Initially you found out about yourself when other people told you about yourself. You are good. You are bad. You are lazy. You are smart. Many sentences about you were handed over to you, some relatively useful, some harmful, and all coming from someone else. Eventually you began to use those same sentences to talk to yourself about yourself in the form of "I statements" like: I am good, I am bad, I am lazy, I am smart, etc.

Did you see what just happened? You just took another person's external experience of you and turned it into an internal conviction about yourself. Your "I" absorbed another person's idea about you into its experience of being. This is where lots of our problems start. As we absorb other people's ideas about us into our own internal experience, our sense of "I" begins to become hopelessly intertwined with the sense of "me."

Over time you will repeat these sentences about yourself over and over again. Each time you do this it is like committing and recommitting yourself to being that person. The momentum of habit that builds as we repeat these "I statements" again and again embeds them more and more into our subjective sense of self. And when other people repeat these sentences about us they are committing us to be that person as well. Eventually we lose track of the sentences, and we just feel like that person and can't imagine any other way to be.

We have just described how our knowledge about ourselves is built out of language, but we don't have to look very far to realize that our knowledge about anything is constructed in language. Any knowledge that we have about anything—including our self—will always be found in the form of sentences in our heads. Without language, it seems, we cannot have knowledge about anything.

Our knowledge about the world and ourselves comes to us through language. It is not direct knowledge of the way things are; it is representational knowledge about the way things are that comes to us in sentences. We just introduced the problems that arise when the sentences about who we are start to be incorporated into our sense of who we are. If we were to expand the scope of this investigation, we would see how many difficulties arise out of the confusion between what we know about things and the reality of the way things are. To fully appreciate the depth of this problem we have to realize that language doesn't just describe reality; it shapes our perception of reality and configures the way we perceive things. What we know about the world shapes how we experience the world. Once again we enter into a strange loop of perception creating itself.

I have heard that Eskimos have twenty-one different words that describe "snow." That means when an Eskimo looks out at the world on a snowy day, he or she sees up to twenty-one different kinds of snow where I see only one. Snow is snow to me, but to him or her there are twenty-one kinds of snow. The snow does not change. If I am standing side by side with an Eskimo on a snowy day, we are in the same world, but our perception of it is totally different. The Eskimo has more possibilities available to him or her than I do because he or she has more distinctions available about the world. If someone were to ask me to point out the different kinds of snow on the ground in front of me, I couldn't do it, but my Eskimo friend could.

Language chops reality into pieces and creates distinctions. These distinctions are incorporated directly into our perception of reality; they become part of how we see the world and ourselves. And the distinctions that we create using language either give us access to greater potentials and possibilities or they limit our access to potentials and possibilities. That is the power of language, for better and for worse. This is so important to understand. The reality that you are seeing right now, both of the outside world and of yourself, and even the fact that you see the two as distinct, is largely shaped by your ideas about reality. You are not simply seeing reality as it is; you are seeing reality as it is being shaped by ideas that you hold about reality.

If we want to gain a more visceral sense of the creative power of language, we need to change the way we think about the sentences we hold in our heads. Rather than thinking about them as statements of fact or as descriptions of what is real, we need to start thinking about them as declarations of commitment. The declarative sentences that we use, either in speech with others or in the form of self-talk in ourselves, are commitments that we make over and over again to what is real. Seen from this perspective we live in a constant effort of committing to a particular reality. The implications of this are that we are not stuck in our current version of reality; we are, in fact, constantly committing ourselves to it. Which means in theory we can change and commit to something else.

There is a transformative power that is released when we start to see the sentences in our heads, and those that we speak, as commitments to reality rather than descriptions of it. If our sentences are descriptions of a reality that already exists, then there is nothing we can do to change it. But if the sentences that I use are commitments that are shaping reality, then those commitments can be reconsidered, and reality can be changed.

We have been taught that language is connected to reality. It is composed of symbols in the form of words that stand for real things. And one of the most profound things about the words that we use to label reality is that they can be passed on to others in the act of communication so that reality can be shared. One of the central occupations of being human is capturing reality in words and then passing it along to each other. Our facility with language is one of the most significant of the factors that allow us to coordinate our efforts and live with the degree of harmony and integration that we currently enjoy. Deepening our capacity to use language will be one of the keys that will make greater harmony and integration between us possible.

There is a downside, however. What underlies the common activity of communication is an almost blind faith in the fact that the words we use to describe reality are an accurate reflection of what reality is. We have already begun to question this assumption. Our language does not necessarily describe a reality that already exists and that we are stuck in. Our language, both in the form of sentences in our own heads and those we use to communicate with others, are actually commitments to a shared view of reality. We are not stuck in reality the way it is. We are actively committing to it. Let's take a deeper look here because seeing that we are not stuck in reality is essential if we are to have any hope of changing it.

When I say to someone, "This is a book," I am committing myself to act in ways that people generally do around books. It is a commitment to certain actions and not others. It means that I might open the book and read it. I might lend it to you, and I might store it on a bookshelf, but I will not boil it in water and try to serve it to you for dinner. The sentence, "This is a book," is a statement of my commitment to act as if this is a book.

Much of reality is more fluid and much less fixed than we have imagined. Our constant affirmation and confirmation of commitments to reality is a big part of what makes things seem so set and unalterable. When we speak with others or think to ourselves, we constantly affirm particular views. We live in a verbal sea of constant affirmation that adheres us to a particular shared view of what is real and true. This background of affirmed commitments is what we use to validate incoming information. If new information aligns with this background of affirmed commitments, we see it as true. If it is misaligned, we either assume it is false, feel compelled to investigate further, or simply don't see it at all.

Circling around to our discussion about self-awareness, I would say that the most compelling language commitment that I know of is the one contained in my name. When someone asks me who I am and I reply, "I am Jeff," what am I committing to? Who is this person Jeff that I am committed to being? Maybe it would be best to think of the sentence, "I am Jeff," not as a description of me, but as my commitment to act like the person I think I am. Then I am free to reconsider my commitment to being that person and consider the possibility that I could be someone else.

To dramatically increase our capacity for change we need to understand how we form our identity or what is called our self-concept. Most of us are trapped in a self-image—a set of ideas that we identify with as who we are. If you want to be free, you have to discover how you are creating your own identity. One useful distinction that will help you in uncovering the mechanisms of self-creation is recognizing the difference between two kinds of thoughts.

The first type of thought appears out of nowhere. These thoughts we commonly refer to as intuitions or inspirations, and we relate to them as thoughts that come to us. The other type of thought appears as self-talk that we relate to as "us" talking to ourselves. When we speak of these thoughts, we assume that this is "us thinking," and we express these thoughts in sentences that start with "I think." Simply put, the distinction is between "just thoughts" versus "me thinking."

Our self is constructed by a never-ending string of conclusions that appear as "me thinking" thoughts. They appear to be us telling ourselves who we are and who we are not. They are statements of limitation. "I am this and not that. I do this and not that." This never-ending set of conclusions creates the sense that there is a boundary around who we are and who we are not. When we look closely, we see that these ideas may be right or wrong, but in themselves they are just ideas, and they do not necessarily dictate who we are or what is real. We realize that we have unknowingly accepted a certain set of unexamined ideas as the limit of who we are.

These limiting ideas create a self-boundary that defines us. Psychologists recognize that some of the thoughts that arise on the inside of the self-boundary are harmful to us. We may have developed habitual thought patterns that tell us that we are stupid, lazy, or worthless, and these cause us to act in destructive or self-destructive ways.

One of the traditional jobs of psychologists is to help us break these unhealthy habitual thought patterns and replace them with healthy ones. It is much better for us to believe that we are intelligent, industrious, and valuable because these thoughts will support us to act in constructive and healthy ways. Psychologists have helped millions of people live much better, more fully integrated lives by pushing unhealthy thought patterns outside of the self boundary and attracting healthier ones into it.

Spiritual practices deal with a different issue. Although a healthy sense of self is better than an unhealthy one, it still limits us to the dictates of thoughts in our heads. We are still left with a sense of being a "something" that is the object of all of the thoughts that we hold about ourselves.

Let's go back for a moment to the question, Who am I? When you ask me who I am and I answer, "I am Jeff," that short sentence stands for me. What I am saying is that I am the entity that this short sentence is about. If I go on to describe myself, I will use a string of sentences, all of which I assume are pointing to me as their object. "I am a teacher." "I am a man." "I am an American." I am a string of sentences that I assume are about me.

An awakening occurs when we let go of all of the sentences in our heads that describe us and realize that we are the one that is aware of those sentences—not the one they are pointing toward. There is no sentence that can capture who you are because you are not a sentence and you are not an object that can be described by a sentence. You are the source of all the sentences in your head, and they can never capture you or hold you in place because you exist before all of them.

Some of the thoughts that we hold are ones that we relate to as optional. Certain thoughts reveal possibilities that I feel free to choose to act on or not. Other thoughts seem to spontaneously lead to action without my being aware of any conscious choice being made. These thoughts simply feel like me. I don't feel like I chose to act on them; the action appears to come directly out of them without my intervention.

What if this were all a function of habit? What if we simply had fallen into an incredibly strong habit of responding to certain thoughts spontaneously as if they were me? And what if that habit had become so strong and so fast that we were no longer aware of doing anything at all? That would make our sense of identity nothing more than a very strong habit of responding to certain parts of our experience spontaneously as if they were me.

If this is true, then it must be possible to break that habit and develop another. To do this we must find a way—for instance, through a spiritual practice like meditation—to break our habit of compulsively identifying with and acting on certain thoughts and feelings. That is when we discover the freedom to make a truly autonomous choice. We feel like a different person. We have the same body and the same mind, but we are free from the compulsive need to be the person that we had known ourselves as before. This degree of freedom opens a doorway to the most profoundly creative act that we can engage in—the act of re-creating our sense of self.

This profound capacity for conscious self-creation is exactly what this book is about. So far, though, we have only explored how our personal sense of self has formed. In the next chapter we need to speak about the deeper cultural self that we are and how that has formed. This is also a self that we learned to be, but it is a self that we share with everyone who grew up in the same culture that we did.

CHAPTER SIX

THE HUMAN FLOW

If you are still reading this book, you have probably already had an awakening beyond the thinking-thing self. These experiences of liberation from the separate sense of self are like removing a psycho-spiritual straightjacket that you never knew you were wearing. For some reason the jacket slipped off, or perhaps you tore it off through painstakingly diligent effort. Either way, you find yourself free from a sense of limitation that had always colored your experience of life. You suddenly feel open, fearless, and unconstrained.

In this chapter we will explore how even our excursions beyond the thinking-thing self are usually interpreted after the fact by the thinking-thing itself. That means we see them not as a vision of a new reality, but as an experience that the thinking-thing has had. In order for our experiences beyond our current sense of self to be truly transformative we must struggle to interpret them in a way that is not limited by the thinking-thing's vantage point. In this chapter we will explore some interpretations that have the power to liberate us into a completely different experience of what it means to be human.

As I have already shared that my own journey into freedom began not as an experience of awakening but as the loss of cosmic connection. As a young boy, I could expand my being until I extended to the edges of the universe, until eventually, as I grew older, I realized that I couldn't anymore. At some point I forgot those early experiences and had no distinct memory of them for a long time. They did not disappear. They were suppressed, into the unconscious, but remained active in my psyche in the form of a persistent spiritual longing that drove me for decades.

Those early childhood experiences resurfaced in a dramatic re-awakening to eternity that I experienced during a retreat that I will describe in more detail in the last chapter of this book. Only then did I have a full memory of those cosmic episodes as a child. From my adult perspective, I saw that my life up to that moment had been completely dedicated to recapturing my early access to universality. Once I opened up again to my true connection to the cosmos it didn't feel like an endpoint; it felt like I had found my way back to the starting line. A long and joyous road of discovery appeared in front of me and I heard the call of a cosmic adventure beckoning me forward. The soul of a new self had captured my imagination and was inviting me to join with others who were similarly called to participate in a dance of unification that would create a new way of being in the world. Our spiritual openings invite us to the profound opportunity of playing our part in awakening this universe to its own True Self.

Our journey through these pages is an exploration of how we can dance together so that our hearts, minds, and bodies can become harmoniously unified into a new way of being. In the previous chapter we painted a picture of the reality that most of us wake up into. We wake up in the midst of an experience of being a separate thing in a world made up of separate things. Our glimpses of unity bring with them a deep recognition of the reality of separation. We become maze-bright, and we want to find our way out of the tangle of assumed isolation.

We gain a little slack in the ties that bind us when we realize that the separate sense of self is not something we were born with. It is something we learned. Our sense of being a particular somebody is created out of reinforced habits that are incorporated into a conceptual sense of self, a self-concept that shapes our perception of the world and of ourselves. We all know habits can be broken and breaking the habit of assumed independent existence *is* what I believe the spiritual path is all about.

A particularly beautiful depiction of an insight beyond separation can be found in a paragraph from the journal of the American Transcendentalist by the feminist genius Margaret Fuller. In it she describes her profound early experience of seeing through the reality of the separate sense of identity.

I remembered how, a little child, I had stopped myself one day on the stairs, and asked, how came I here? How is it that I seem to be this Margaret Fuller? What does it mean? What shall I do about it? I remembered all the times and ways in which the same thought had returned. I saw how long it must be before the soul can learn to act under these limitations of time and space, and human nature; but I saw, also, that it Must do it, — that it must make all this false true, — and sow new and immortal plants in the garden of God; before it could return again. I saw there was no self; that selfishness was all folly, and the result of circum- stance; that it was only because I thought self real that I suffered; that I had only to live in the idea of the All, and all was mine.

When we awaken from the separate sense of self we are faced with a very perplexing question. We lived our entire life until that moment under the assumption that we knew who we were; suddenly we find that that person does not exist. We thought we were a particular someone who had a unique set of characteristics and was making choices and living a life. Now we see that there is no such person. As Margaret Fuller said, "There is no such self."

So we find ourselves compelled to ask, who am I? Another way to ask the same question that I found particularly impactful on my own journey came from the spiritual teacher Da Free John who asked, "Do you know who is living your life?"

From the quote above Margaret Fuller seems to have discovered that it was possible to live from 'the All.'

This is the promise of mystical traditions the world over. Once we discover that we are not the separate sense of self we can surrender to the wisdom and compassion of universal being and allow it to live through us. Traditionally the goal of mystical life is to let go of the illusion of a separate self and surrender to the will of God, Goddess, or Divinity in some form.

This traditional view recognizes two modes of being – that of the separate sense of self or ego, and that of a soul surrendered to higher consciousness. But a close examination of our experience reveals that there are other modes of being that co-exist between the life of the isolated ego and the life of the God realized saint. These in-between modes of being are collective patterns of behavior, or what I call currents of being, that are held not inside us but flow between us. We are all caught in many different currents of being that manifest through us as choices that we falsely assume we are independently making. It is more accurate to say that collective currents of being are living through us disguised as lives created by individual choices.

Awakening to the collective currents of being that are living through us is profoundly liberating. We find that so many of the things we have done were not an expression of authentic choice. They were an expression of cultural preferences and assumptions that simply acted themselves out through us while we were asleep in the dream of independent existence. Now that we are awake to these currents we discover a new dimension of autonomy and we begin to have the power to choose which currents of being we live into and which we leave behind. Most profoundly, some of us awaken to an emergent current of being full of goodness and promise that we can allow to manifest through us.

At first blush this may seem upsetting as if it diminishes our independence. After all no one wants to discover that their choices are merely a reflection of cultural values and social norms. On the other hand, discovering the depth to which we are a manifestation of collective currents opens up a miraculous possibility. By becoming more authentically awake to the full spectrum of our interdependence we can liberate ourselves from blind adherence to the currents of collective being and engage together in an effort to generate a new current that can uplift all of humanity. Inspiring people to participate in the creation of a new current of being is my primary purpose in writing this book.

In this chapter we will explore how a self is best thought of as a collective current of being that we are all caught in. By the end of this book we will see how the new current of being that reveals itself in our deepest spiritual realizations is much more than a new set of cultural values or social norms. It is the soul of a new self in the process of being born. It is asking to be allowed into our hearts and minds so that it can reorganize life at a higher level of love.

To begin our exploration of the collective currents of being that live through us we need to return briefly to the distinction between the "I" and the "me." As we have already said we wake up to find ourselves encased in a sense of self that is an amalgamation of two elements. There is the mysterious source of awareness that we call "I," and the self-concept made up of everything we think we know about who we are that we call "me". The source of our awareness and the identity formed by our ideas about ourselves have become jumbled into a confusing experience of selfhood. We wake up into this confusion. Confusion about who we are at an existential level is one of the first signs of awakening. If you experience that confusion, embrace it with the confidence of knowing you can move beyond it.

Our self-concept is the objective experience that we have of ourselves. It is our experience of "me." Those who engage in deep spiritual practices like meditation sometimes recognize that the self-concept is an illusion. There is no self. There is a vast and ever-changing array of experiences and ideas that merge together to create an impression or sense that there is a thing called a self that is who we are, but that sense of self is not real.

The self-concept or the "me" is made up of layers of experience and beliefs about that experience. We have already looked at what you could call the personal self or the personality. The personality is your experience of, and ideas about, who you think you are. My personality is of being Jeff, who was born in the United States in 1964. I have a particular family and lived through a particular set of events and circumstances. My history has shaped my personality, and my personality is largely unique to me because I am the only one who lived exactly my life.

It is not only my personal history, however, that has shaped me. I am not just an expression of my personal history. I am also shaped by layers of cultural history.

Recently I was traveling in Paris, and I found that no matter how hard I tried, it always seemed that I was speaking more loudly than anyone around me—unless they were Americans. Speaking loudly is part of my cultural conditioning.

When we travel outside of the culture we are raised in, we feel our cultural conditioning strongly. We might never become aware of these aspects of our selves unless we leave our culture, because everyone we meet within our own culture shares them.

A number of intersecting cultural influences shape each of us. We are part of a family. There are characteristics that families have as a whole that each individual member of the family will express to some degree or another.

We belong to different social circles. We are part of a circle of friends and might belong to a professional group. The cultures shared in these groups influence how we experience ourselves and how we show up in the world. Have you ever had a friend who started spending time with a new group of friends and started to change in ways you didn't like? You might have wished that they would stop associating with that group because of how they were being influenced.

We are all profoundly shaped by the cultural influences of the different groups we are a part of. Those groups can be as small and close as a family or as large and expansive as a nation. The different cultures that we participate in, from the very small to the very large, all shape who we are.

This level of cultural influence is commonly understood. Seeing the cultural shaping of national identity or social circles is not likely to be new information to you, but there is a much more profound level of cultural influence shaping us that is almost never questioned. It comes from the one culture that anyone reading this book is likely to be a part of. It is the culture of the Western world.

Who we experience ourselves to be at the deepest level has been shaped through the history of the Western world. Some of the broad strokes of that history include an intellectual heritage from ancient Greece that was absorbed into the Roman Empire and blended with Judeo-Christian theology during the Middle Ages. The Middle Ages gave way to the Age of Reason, initially through the Italian Renaissance and later during the European Enlightenment. The Enlightenment gave rise to the modern world where we currently find ourselves.

The sense of self that we have inherited from this historical journey is the experience of being a thinking-thing—a thing that thinks and chooses to act. Our deepest experience of being human is of being a thing that thinks and acts, and this sense of self has been constructed, refined, and solidified throughout the development of Western culture until now. Everyone in Western influenced cultures is born with it. One of the miraculous spiritual realizations we can have is that this foundational layer of conditioning can be undercut. We can see through the perceptual habits that shape our experience into a thinking-thing. When we do, we will not know who or what we are. We will be free of the limitations of a recognizable self-concept, and we will be available to be reorganized around a new sense of self.

If we had been born in the Middle Ages, we would not have been born into the experience of being a thinking-thing. People at that time did not necessarily experience themselves as things that think and choose to act. Instead they experienced spirits and demons acting through them. When someone did terrible things, they were not punished because it was believed that they had chosen to do bad things. It was believed that some demonic force or evil spirit had possession of their soul, and it—or they—needed to be expelled. Try to imagine what your experience of self would be if you experienced your actions originating in spirits that acted through you rather than through choices that you made.

Our cognitive inheritance from the Western Enlightenment has blessed us with what I like to call things-in-space consciousness. That consciousness sees reality as an infinite expanse of three-dimensional space populated by things that act upon each other. Recognizing how deeply we are influenced by culture can undermine, in a positive way, our confidence in our independent existence. Traveling to other cultures allows us to see how profoundly shaped we are by the culture of our origin. This, for some, is experienced as a tremendously liberating experience, but, and this is the point of this chapter, the realization of cultural levels of being is usually still interpreted from the vantage point of the thinking-thing. That means when we think about how culture influences us, we still tend to imagine ourselves to be a thing that exists in culture. And we imagine culture itself to be made up of a collection of other things—attitudes, ideas, and artifacts—that act upon us. More often than not our experiences outside of our culture of origin do nothing to challenge our fundamental sense of self because we still habitually relate to those experiences in terms of being a thing that exists in a culture that influences us.

What way of thinking about being human could undermine our confidence in being a thinking-thing? One alternative I would ask you to consider is to think of humanity not as a collection of entities, but as a flow of activity that runs through culture the way ripples run across the surface of water. What if we are not things that think and decide to act? What if there are simply mental and physical changes that run through culture through the activity of our lives? When we say "human being," we assume we are talking about a thing. What if by "human being" we meant a way of being, a flow of activity, and not a collection of individual entities?

When I was a child, I had an electronic football game. It was a toy football field made of metal with little plastic football players on it. When you turned it on, the whole game vibrated, and the little plastic football players shuffled all over the playing surface, which was painted to look like a football field. When I looked at those little football players shuffling around, I imagined that they were running plays. I saw little beings deciding to run through openings in their opponents and tackle each other. In my mind they were tiny players all making choices about how to run, turn, or stop. In reality there was an electronic motor that was vibrating a playing surface and making all the plastic figures on it move about.

In the same way there are cultural flows, like asking "How are you?" when you greet someone, that are really a part of culture and that flow through the individuals in that culture. We are caught in an elaborate story about our independent and isolated existence as thinking-things when in fact there is always a flow that organizes what we do and what we think. There are more localized flows that flow into more expanded flows, which in turn flow into even more expanded flows, and so on. Society is a mass of human flows organized in particular ways to result in certain behavioral and perceptual possibilities and not others.

When you are at home, you are in one flow, at work another, walking on the street yet another. The activity of any flow is governed by your interactions with other people and with the culturally created objects that exist within the circumstances of the flow. Think about how you spend your time at work. What do you tend to think about there? What kinds of conversations do you tend to have, and what do you do? Then imagine the way you are when you are in a meeting—the actions, speech, and thought of that flow. Compare that to the flow that occurs during a coffee break, or when you are on the highway driving home from work, or when you are at home.

Human life is made up of flows of action, speech, and thought. If you think of the different flows that occur in your life, you will feel how they constrain you. It takes effort to act in ways that go against the flow. It takes very little effort to work within the flow. In fact it happens more or less automatically. Each flow of your life flows into the next, and the next, and then back again. If you can embrace this perspective deeply enough, you will start to see that humanity is a flow of being rather than a collection of independent-acting agents. Human being is an energetic flow that occurs between individual humans and in our engagement with the world.

The human flow of action, speech, and thought is influenced and held in our interactions with each other and the objects that we create. You get up in the morning and walk out of the bedroom through the door. You then go to the second-floor bathroom using the stairs. Once in the bathroom you clean your teeth with a toothbrush and toothpaste. The phone rings, and you pick up the receiver, place it to your mouth, and say "hello." You pick up your car keys, get in your car, and drive to work.

That whole flow of activity was constantly being reinforced by interactions with the created objects that govern the human flow. You never get up in the morning and climb out the window. You never clean your teeth with a towel, and when the phone rings you never put the receiver to your elbow when you speak. Our interactions with the objects of the world are governed by habitual ways of being that are passed along to us from culture and that we in turn pass along to others. We need not think about our interactions within an established flow because they are so habitual that they flow out of us without any conscious thought on our part.

The objects in our world and the social conventions attached to them define different flows of appropriate activity. We are moved by these flows as much and often even more than we are choosing to act. The deeper point here is that we have been trained to think of ourselves as choosing agents—thinking-things—and that way of thinking is not a reflection of who we ultimately are. In fact that way of thinking and all of the associated behaviors and perceptions associated with it is a cultural flow that we are caught in.

The twentieth-century German philosopher Martin Heidegger described the habitual way of being human as acting out the behaviors of the "One." According to Heidegger, most of the time without realizing it we are not acting authentically. We are simply doing what one does in any given situation. To become truly authentic we must wake up from the dream of the One and begin to consciously choose to live our lives. I am simply extending this insight to our fundamental experience of ourselves. Our experience of ourselves is a perceptual habit. We perceive ourselves and others as thinking-things because that is a deep cultural flow that we are caught in. Most people live their whole lives without ever seeing beyond this habit, without ever achieving maze brightness at this profound depth. I assume that those of you reading this book have seen beyond the maze to some degree and together we have the opportunity to participate in establishing a new flow of being human.

The flows of our life are molded by our interactions with the world, and the most significant interactions we have are with other people. Our interactions with others are constantly shaping the flow of activity, speech, and thought that we exist inside of. We act certain ways with certain people in certain circumstances. We act one way when we are in a stadium watching a football game and another way at a funeral. Each of these situations has a unique human flow. And we are all adept at "getting in the flow." If you go to either a football game or a funeral for the first time, it won't take long before you learn how to be simply by watching and imitating others.

We live in constant, unconscious communication with those around us. The American sociologist George Herbert Mead called this level of communication the conversation of gestures. We are constantly gesturing to each other. We reinforce with gesture how to be in any given situation. We ourselves act in certain ways that fall within the bounds of cultural norms, and we communicate wordlessly, often without being aware that we are, instructions that hold others in what we have learned is the most appropriate way of being.

Go into some completely new social situation, and very quickly without needing to talk to anyone you will begin to get into the flow. If you walk into a football stadium for the first time, you will inevitably sit in your seat and look down at the playing field because that is what everyone around you is gesturing to do. You are very unlikely to stand up and turn away from the field, at least for very long. If you do, the conversation of gesture will get louder until people start demanding that you get into the flow. Polite society has some tolerance for coloring outside of the lines, but if you go too far, for too long, you will find yourself on the other side of strong directives or in prison.

We are part of a human flow. Most of our actions are more the result of habitual adherence to social norms than they are independent, conscious choices on our part. To an extent much greater than we imagine, or perhaps would like to imagine, we are vehicles through which social norms and customs flow. These social norms pass through us like waves passing through water. Many of our actions are nothing more than the movement of cultural flows. Rather than define a human being as an acting agent, we might want to define human being as a particular collection of culturally reinforced ways of being.

One of the deepest culturally reinforced habits of being is the strong habit of associating our actions with some entity called me. Whenever I act, I habitually assume that some entity that I call Jeff decided to initiate the action. Not only do I habitually assume that my actions originate in an entity called me, but everyone around me also assumes that my actions originate from an entity called me. When I do something offensive, the people who are offended will hold some imagined entity called Jeff responsible for the offending action. They will assume that Jeff did something offensive, and they will respond to him from this assumption. When I do something that makes people happy, they will thank me because they see me as the source of that happiness.

Everyone we meet will treat us as if we are a thinking-and-choosing entity. This will constantly reinforce this perception in ourselves. Those who know me personally will not only treat me as an entity, but also as a particular entity named Jeff that has unique characteristics. They will expect me to act in certain ways that they have come to associate with me being Jeff, and when I act out of character they will respond to let me know by telling me that I am not acting like "myself."

There is a "chicken and egg" question here. Which came first? Was there an individual being that became part of a culture, or was there a culture that created an individual being?

We have already discussed how my identity as Jeff is a habit of identifying certain thoughts, feelings, and actions as belonging to an imagined entity that exists somewhere inside my body. We might assume that this habit is something that I hold personally and that others hold about me, but there is another way to look at it. What if we think of culture as an organic whole rather than a collection of individuals? Culture then is more like a collective entity—a being. Culture, not individuals, holds a conception about what it means to be human, and the actions that occur in that culture continually reflect and reinforce that idea of being human. Human being lives in culture, not in individuals.

Within the culture, individuals and the ideas they hold about themselves and each other are in a constant state of interaction with other individuals and their ideas.

This constant interaction results in the manifestation of certain behaviors and not others. We are cultural beings as much, if not more, than we are individuals. We are the natural outcome of ideas about being human held by the culture we were born into. If we insert new ideas about what it means to be human into culture, we will show up differently and give birth to a new way of being human. The transformation that we need now is not individual; it is collective. We need more than a shift in personal identity; we need to shift the cultural norm of what it means to be human.

We are largely cultural beings. Human beings are not individual, separate entities. Human being is a way of being that is held in culture and emerges through individuals. We are a collective being. In fact, even our self-awareness is not something we possess as individuals. We think of ourselves as self-aware, but the capacity to reflect back on our self is not something we could develop as an individual. It is a collective capacity that was developed through interactions between us. Self-awareness doesn't arise in individuals. It manifests as a group phenomenon. Self-awareness is a characteristic of culture that expresses itself through individuals.

Imagine that you were the only human being on earth. You could learn things. You could learn what was safe to eat and what made you sick. You might learn where to find food and how to store it. You might learn how to hunt, how to avoid danger, and how to find shelter in all kinds of weather. You could become very intelligent through trial and error, but you would not learn to think in words or self-reflect.

Language emerges as an interaction between people. Our understanding of ourselves as a being that has a name is something we first learn through communication with others, and then it becomes internalized and solidified in the self-communication of thought. Eventually the habit of talking to ourselves about ourselves becomes so ingrained in us that we hardly notice it. We lose track of this self-talk, and it simply becomes absorbed into our experience of ourselves. Eventually the things we think about ourselves become fused with our perception of ourselves.

We have learned to experience ourselves as a specific thinking-thing, in my case as Jeff. We see ourselves as acting agents in the world, as beings and entities. To liberate ourselves from this flow and become available to initiate a new one, we must take a radically impersonal view of human life. We must see the actions coming through us, me typing and you reading, as the manifestation of personal and cultural flows of being. To clarify this view even further, we need to see that human activity is a continuous response to shifts in the circumstances that surround us rather than as the consequences of decisions made by willing agents. This discussion is an intermediate step on the path that leads to the embrace of true authenticity.

Think of a stream of activity that is governed solely by habit. There is no doer that is guiding action; there are just habits that have been learned over time. These habits of activity developed in response to encounters with different circumstances. As we continually engage with the environment, that ongoing encounter stimulates the growth of habits of action, thought, and emotion. As long as there is no disharmony between the environment and our habitual ways of acting, thinking, and feeling, we remain essentially unconscious.

Think about how you get up in the morning. Most of us get out of bed, make coffee, take a shower, get dressed, and leave the house in the morning without really being aware of any of it actually happening. The whole process is simply a manifestation of habit.

Now, what happens if just before we leave the house we reach into our coat pocket and realize we don't have our car keys? At that point we wake up and become aware of the circumstances around us. Something is out of place. There is a disruption of habit that awakens us to consciousness and initiates the self-conscious and deliberate activity of searching for our keys. We will remain in this awakened state of consciousness until we find our keys. Then we can get back into our unthinking routine, and the harmonious union of habit and environment has been restored.

The American philosopher John Dewey wrote at length about how impeding the harmonious routine of our habitual ways of being sparks an impulse to urgency, immediacy, and directionality. The disruption of our routines wakes us up to an impulse that is directed toward some possible future, in this example, the future possibility is driving your car to work.

Once awake, we feel compelled to restore the harmony between habit and activity in service of realizing our directive. The awakened impulse in human beings initiates a process of deliberation in which our minds make predictions about possible outcomes of different courses of action. When a course of action seems to promise the satisfactory restoration of harmony, that action manifests through us. If harmony is restored, we merge again into the stream of activity. In the case of having lost our keys, we immediately start to imagine different places where we could look for them and search where it seems most promising to find them. Once we find our keys, we walk out the door and continue unconsciously to work until our next encounter with disharmony.

This all happens without the need to assume the existence of any "ego" or "self" that is a willful agent making decisions and choosing to act. Life is simply an impulse that continually seeks to maintain harmonious union of habit and environment in service of some intended aim. Human beings are simply enacting life's continuous quest to maintain harmony in service of the future.

In the most profound sense we wake up in the middle of a routine of being a human being. Something disrupted that routine. Perhaps it was an awakening experience, or the loss of an awakening experience, or simply an event that stopped our forward movement in life. Something woke us up from the dream of being a thinking-thing. That disruption creates disharmony that initiates a search for a new understanding of what it means to be human. There will always be a temptation to find some quick solution that restores harmony so that we can return to the unconsciousness of routine. If we resist this temptation, we can remain awake.

If we are lucky enough to wake up in the first place, and bold enough to remain awake, we can abide in freedom outside of the routine of being human. If we can find others who are living in that freedom, together we can re-create the world. We have a foothold in a reality beyond the normal, and we can use that footing as leverage to enact authentic change.

Seeing how our sense of self has been shaped by personal and cultural influences can be a step on the road that leads beyond the limitations of the thinking-thing self. To go all the way into a new paradigm, however, I would say that we still have to take that inquiry beyond any assumption of being a thinking-thing that is being shaped. This is very challenging because anytime we think, we have to use language and when we are thinking this far beyond our normal experience we find that language tends to work against us.

Our current language was built in the same things-in-space consciousness that we are attempting to move beyond and it often drags us back into that consciousness over and over again. The dominant level of consciousness in any culture has a powerful gravitational attraction that continually pulls us back home every time we stray. We are caught in a current of being and attempting to contemplate our way out of it so that we can generate a different current of being to live in. If you find this inquiry difficult don't be surprised. It is.

As we have seen, our foundational sense of self, our bottom-line experience of being human, has taken shape through the course of Western history. This core experience of selfhood is what we want to question and ultimately shift. Any change at this level of our identity will dramatically shift how all of life on Earth is lived because human beings and our current sense of self profoundly influence existence on this planet. The possibility that this book is dedicated to is shifting the experience of being human in such a way that we are able to meet the global challenges we face and move into an unimaginably positive planetary and ultimately universal future.

When our experience of being human changes, all of human consciousness changes with it. If we are only able to change at more superficial levels of identity, if we alter certain aspects of our personality or expand beyond our nationalistic value system, for instance, we will change some elements and characteristics of our consciousness, but the foundation of it will remain the same. It is hard to imagine that anything less than a foundational shift in consciousness will lead to the degree of change that many of us intuit is demanded by these challenging times.

When a shift at this depth takes place everything changes. It is not just that we are seeing something new. We are seeing from some place new. Experiences of this type can be frightening, but they are also exhilarating because they reveal an unimaginable potential for growth and transformation—not just for us but also for all of humanity. As the French novelist Marcel Proust said:

The real voyage of discovery consists not in seeking new lands but seeing with new eyes.

Those of us who have experienced even short-lived shifts at this depth of selfhood will attest to the fact that they do not feel like shifts in personality. They don't feel like a new experience of being you. They feel like a different experience of being human. They can even feel like an experience beyond what we would normally consider being human. This book is an inquiry designed to unseat our current sense of self and open us up to a different possibility of being.

As we contemplate the personal and cultural influences that have shaped us we will naturally tend to think from the vantage point of the thinking-thing. That means we will imagine an individual who has been shaped by cultural influences. Do you see how that view is still embedded in an assumption of being an individual? It is this very assumption that we are working to unseat. Over and over again we will see that even our efforts to unseat this assumption are bound in the assumption. The paradox we are faced with is that we are on a contemplative journey aimed at liberating us from self-concept, and yet the only platform we have to engage that contemplation with is our self-concept.

We have already determined that there was no individual, no "me," there at the start. The individual who experiences him- or herself as having been shaped by personal history and culture is itself a self-concept and not an actual entity. When we awaken beyond cultural influence we tend to see ourselves as a thing that had previously been shaped by the winds of cultural forces. But we are not a thing. So we cannot be a thing that gets shaped by culture. What I want to do now is take us on a journey into a way of thinking that gives us a glimpse of a very different way of imagining reality than what we have been taught.

We experience ourselves as conscious things that decide to act—thinking-things. Consider it for a moment. Right now you experience yourself to be a thing, a being that has decided to read this book and is choosing to continue reading it right now. The experience of being a thing that thinks and acts is so central to our view of reality that we can hardly imagine anything different.

There is a different way of thinking that flips everything upside-down. Rather than thinking about an individual who has been shaped by cultural elements, think about a culture that has been shaped into the experience of being an individual. In the next chapter we will begin a journey into this new way of thinking that will build through the rest of this book into a new conception of reality and a new understanding of being human. When we engage in this new way of thinking we have to move slowly and carefully because the gravity of things-in-space consciousness will exert a relentless pressure on us pulling us back into thinking-thing shape. I am sure if you have gotten this far you are up for the challenge.

CHAPTER SEVEN

REDISTRIBUTING THE SELF

In the last two chapters we developed a picture of the self that calls into question all of our assumptions about some actually existing entity that is the agent of our actions and the source of our choices. Instead we explored a view in which we— whatever we are— became habituated into believing that we were a self and then acting as if that were the case for so long that we couldn't see things any other way. Everyone we know shares this experience of learned selfhood, and so we seldom if ever question the reality of it. We assume we are a self and act as if we are, and we assume everyone else is too, and everyone else constantly reinforces that belief by acting like a separate self and treating us like one.

The thinking-thing self is a habituated belief. It is the belief that we are an entity with a name and a history and the ability to think and choose to act. The self is not a thing. It is not who we are. It is not an entity that lives inside of us. The self is a belief or, as we will soon see, an organizing principle.

We have been exploring the self as a cultural habit that enacts itself through individuals. This is a dramatically different view than we have generally been taught, but even a notion this radical will be claimed by the thinking-thing self. Without realizing it, we most likely will see culture as a collection of thoughts shared by individuals who habitually believe them. If we do, the separate self is still the reference point.

In the current chapter we will gently allow ourselves to let go of any sense of separation. If we follow this path with all our heart, we will not be able to avoid falling deeply into the wormhole of a new reality, because if it is true that we live in a continuous reality that does not have any breaks or gaps, then nothing can be limited by time or space. Nothing could exist now and not then, here and not there. Everything exists everywhere always. We must hold this unlimited perspective when considering the nature of self. The self cannot be limited by time or space. It exists everywhere always.

Anyone who has experienced the truly unbounded nature of self will have recognized that there is no self in the way that we have been trained to believe. There is no individual "me" that exists separate from the rest of reality. Even thinking of the self as a habituated way of being human is most likely going to be interpreted in terms of ideas held in common by separate individuals. I believe we have to go further than this in order to fully appreciate the magnitude of what we are being called to as the generating elements of a new self.

When we think of shifting into a new sense of self, we can't help but think in terms of us shifting, but that is not the way this shift happens. You don't let go of one sense of self and pick up another. The sense of self is not something that you have. It is not something that can be let go of and replaced. You are not a thing that has a sense of self to let go of. You are not a thing. You do not exist as a separate entity that thinks and chooses and has an identity. There is no being called Jeff.

The reason that we have to go this far is so that we can completely unhinge ourselves from our current conception of reality. The phrase "You can't get there from here" comes to mind. You are currently thinking from inside of a thinking-thing self. You have no choice about it. You experience yourself as a thing that thinks. That experience limits reality. Earlier we defined the self as a platform of perception. It is something you stand on and perceive from like an observation deck. If you are standing on an observation deck, you can only see the view from that platform of perception. You can't see the view from the ground up there, and you can't see the view from a higher platform either. If you live inside of a thinking-thing belief system, you can only think about and perceive reality like a thinking-thing.

The next sense of self will not emerge out of our current world. We have already explored why the sense of self and the world it emerges out of cannot be separated. They represent a necessary unity. They mutually define each other. You can't have an inside without an outside. You can't have an above without a below. And you can't have a self without a world, or a world without a self.

The world we know is the world of the thinking-thing self. The new self will arise within a new world. Everything has to change at once. A completely new experience of reality will be born, and we—in the form of the thinking-thing self that we have known ourselves to be—will not be there to witness it. We are like a ball of yarn that thinks it will be there after the unraveling. We will not be there after the unraveling of the self. We are the self that will be unraveled. We are the dream of separation that the new self will wake up from. We are not the dreamer. We are the dream.

This does not mean that there is no continuity between the current experience of reality and the next. Reality is subjective. It is experienced. There is a universal subjectivity that gives this universe life. That universal subjectivity is currently caught in a dream of separation. We are that dream. The true source of awareness that is absolute subjectivity will wake up from the dream. When it does, our current identity will not be there to witness it. A new self is not going to awaken in us, in this world. A new world containing a new self will appear simultaneously as one. We will be that, but we won't recognize ourselves.

There is one thing that I want to be clear about: the absolute subjectivity that is the source of life in this reality will be the source of life in the next as well. So in a sense we will be there—not as the separate self, but as that absolute subjectivity. In order to deeply grasp these very extraordinary ideas, we need to go on a journey together. We will need to contemplate the nature of unity, continuity, non-separation, and the absolute. We will also need to revisit the distinction between the "I" and the "me" to see how the sense of separate identity that we have believed ourselves to be becomes manifest within an ocean of undifferentiated subjectivity.

We can start this contemplation by thinking about continuity and our experience of time. We are trained to think in terms of chunks of time. Our things-in-space consciousness relates to time as if it were made up of distinct and separate moments that add up to hours, days, weeks, and years.

If time is composed of separate moments, then how does any knowledge of one moment find its way into the next? How do I know anything about the past if past moments are truly separate from the present?

We commonly imagine that moments pass over and through us—or that we pass through them. Either way we are taking the position of being a thing that exists in time. As soon as we do that, we reinforce the same things-in-space consciousness that we are attempting to liberate ourselves from, because we see time as something separate from us that we exist inside of.

The American philosopher William James articulated a different and, I believe, much more interesting way to think about time. Time is continuous with no breaks or gaps. Time is continuous. This means that time is eternal, and each moment contains all previous and all future moments. All of time is contained in the present. Time is a unified whole.

Our experience can be imagined to fit on a bell curve that measures intensity of awareness. The peak of the bell curve is the present moment. Our awareness of reality builds to peak intensity in the present moment and then fades into the past. This means that in our experience of the present there is a tail that runs back to the beginning of time. It also means that all future moments have tails that are passing through this one. In effect this moment has a leading edge that reaches forward to the end of time. The further from the present an experienced moment is, the dimmer our awareness of it.

It is critical to understand that the tail back to the beginning of time and the leading edge that reaches to the end of time both exist in this present moment. When we are in some future moment, we are not in a different moment. We will still be right here in this moment, the only moment that there is. It is just that the intensity of awareness will have shifted focus, so another part of this moment will feel like the present.

At the height of the bell curve of perception we experience the present moment as immediately, intensely available and vivid. Because of this intensity the experience of the present feels like now. I am sitting in a coffee shop typing. The experience of my fingers striking the keys feels like now. The woman behind the counter feels like she is here with me now. When I think of my walk to get here, it feels like then. It is not as vivid to my mind, so it feels like the past. When I think about what I might do tomorrow, it feels like the future is dim and indistinct.

Our experience of time is an interpretation of reality based on our human experience of it. The present feels like "now" because of the intensity of the experience of it. The past and the future feel like "then" because they are less vivid and available. The past, present, and future are all experienced now, as they currently exist in this moment. This moment is eternal, containing all of time.

Our experience of this eternal moment fluctuates; the focus of awareness shifts; but it does not go anywhere. We imagine that time passes because we have constructed a belief about reality based on the fluctuations that actually always happen in the present.

In our normal interpretation of time we think of past moments as existing somewhere other than here, accessible to us only in the form of memories stored in our brains. If this were true and past moments were no longer present, where are they? What happens to them once they have lived their fleeting existence?

If reality is eternal, then there is no need to imagine either that the past exists in some realm other than here, or that it is dead and gone. In eternity, the past is not just a memory of something no longer here; it is the current experience of something that is no longer the focus of awareness. We are tuning in to that part of the present that is the past. Similarly, when we envision the future, we are not imagining ideas about a future that exists out there; we are experiencing budding future moments as they currently exist in the present.

Whether this interpretation of time is true or not is immaterial. What matters is that it gives us access to a different conception of time. Unfortunately, any conceivable notion of time, even our conception of eternal time, becomes inextricably bound in our image of ourselves as thinking-things. In order for something to be conceivable to us in our current form, it has to be retrofitted to our image of ourselves as organisms that have minds. If an idea does not fit within that image, it is unintelligible to us. This has always been the challenge of truly transformative ideas. If an idea is truly not of this consciousness, it cannot be directly understood by this consciousness. It can only be gestured toward indirectly. Then we follow in the direction being pointed toward in the hopes of falling into a different experience of consciousness. This is one of the wormhole inquiries I mentioned earlier, designed to hold our attention near the edge of a spiritual wormhole to increase our chances of falling through.

Once we start envisioning the unity of one aspect of our experience, like time, we realize that we cannot separate that from other parts of reality. If we are continuous through time, we must also be continuous in space. If there is no now and then, there can't be a here and there either. Contemplating the nature of non-separation leads to the realization of non-separation. Nothing is separate. Nothing is divisible. All is one. We live inside of a unity that has no parts, no gaps, and no separation.

Everything is smeared throughout existence. Everything is here now. The recognition that reality is both immediate and infinite has been discovered in deep spiritual practices like meditation for millennia. It is also a view that is explored today in the philosophical idea of hyperobjects coined by Timothy Morton of Rice University.

A hyperobject is an unbounded entity. Morton is most concerned with the recognition that global warming is a hyperobject, which means that it is immediately present everywhere. The unbounded nature of hyperobjects makes them the unavoidable context for all of life. We cannot escape them. They are always immediately present everywhere, whether we are aware of them or not. Throughout the remainder of this book I will use this term liberally and perhaps at times extend its reach beyond what Morton himself might.

The thinking-thing self is a hyperobject, and the new Self beyond the thinking-thing self will also be a hyperobject. It is not a self that can be limited to any particular time or location. It does not exist inside of any individual or group of individuals. It is immediately present always and everywhere. It is the unavoidable context of life.

The challenge we face now is to get a glimpse of a self that is not limited in any way from inside the boundary of being an individual. I want to suggest that the fundamental obstacle to the realization of a new Self is an unconscious assumption that we all have. That assumption is the belief that we are having an experience of reality. This is the root cause of our sense of separation.

We have been deeply indoctrinated into a belief that we are in contact with the world through our senses, taking in information that is turned into a picture of the world that we experience. We imagine that a memory of the past is like a movie that was stored in our mind to be viewed later. We imagine that when we envision the future we are generating images of possibilities that we could strive toward. When we look out at the scene in front of us, we believe that we are looking at a picture of reality that is presented to us by our minds. When we discover that things are not the way they appeared to be, we don't assume that reality changed; we assume that we had misconstrued reality. We don't assume that we are seeing reality as it is necessarily because we know we are seeing through our minds and our minds can misinterpret reality.

As we have been exploring, we unconsciously assume that we are a thing that moves through time gathering information about each passing moment, storing that information as memory, imagining and living into different possible futures. We are a thinking-thing that experiences a reality that we are living inside of but are separate from. This entire construct has to go if we are to experience a radically different possibility.

To see through such a profoundly conditioned relationship to life takes tremendous concentrated attention and a huge heart. In my life the practice of meditation has been a vehicle for explosive journeys beyond the assumption of separation. In deep meditation I can let it all go, everything. I can allow my sense of being separate to dissolve and disappear. Reality returns to what it truly is—an ongoing cascade of experience.

In deep meditation there is no me experiencing reality. There is just a flow of experience that includes periodic experiences of feeling like a thing that experiences reality. Reality is a dazzling fluctuation of perception. Everything, everything, everything is another experience. There is no me experiencing reality, and there is no reality being experienced. There is just experience. My sense of self is not a self; it is an experience of being a self. The contemplation that we are engaged in right now is not "a" contemplation. It is not an activity that I am engaged in. It is an experience of being someone who is engaged in the activity of contemplating.

If we in our thinking-thing delusion try to imagine a new Self, we find it impossible. Our current sense of self cannot imagine its successor. Luckily it doesn't have to.

The thinking-thing doesn't need to imagine its successor. The thinking-thing is not on a journey into its next incarnation. The thinking-thing simply needs to step aside and allow reality to reconfigure itself around a new conception of self. The next self-sense is not going to be constructed by thinking-things; it is going to grow out of the ground of reality like a tree grows out of the ground of the earth.

We are not a thinking-thing. The experience of being a thinking-thing is inherent in the current configuration of reality. Experience is the "stuff" of reality, and we are made of that. We are not a thing having an experience; we are an experience of being a thing. Or even more accurately, there are no things having experiences of reality; there is simply a cascade of experience that includes experiences of being things.

The metaphor I like to use for this is an eddy in a river current. When we see an eddy in a river, what we are seeing is a small whirlpool. It looks like a circular swirl. We call it an eddy. It is a thing with a name, but we know that it is not really a thing. We could not take the eddy out of the river and hold it in our hand. If we tried to scoop the eddy out of the river, all we would end up with is a handful of water. The eddy is not a thing separate from the water. It is a particular organization of water. Visually we can see it as separate from the water, but in reality it is not separate.

The self is the same. In the vast play of human interaction there are recognizable selves, but you cannot separate them from the field of human interaction itself. The self is a particular organization of human activity and interaction. It cannot be separated from the field of human activity and interaction any more than an eddy can be separated from the water.

The self is an organizing principle that shapes human activity around the belief that we are separate things having an independent experience of reality. That experience of being separate is the core of the current sense of self. It is a hyperobject. It is the unavoidable context for all of life. It shapes all of our perceptions and all of our actions. It is the God we worship. It is the creator of life as we know it. It is responsible for all of the greatness of the human world and all of the tragedy. It has had a long run as the supreme being, and now it is time for it to step down from power, allowing space for the next self to emerge and completely reconfigure reality.

Examining other organizing principles in nature will help us understand the depth and significance of what we are envisioning. Gravity is a magnificent organizing principle. It is a hyperobject. I am looking at the tabletop in front of me. There are a number of objects on it. They all sit still on top of the table. Gravity holds them down onto the table. If there were no gravity, everything would float away. The way all physical objects are arranged in the world is governed by gravity. If the organizing principle of gravity were to disappear, we would live in a very different world.

Now let's look at a human system, say a basketball game. If you look out at a basketball game, you can see immediately that there is an organizing principle involved. The rules of the game are the organizing principles. The players stay on the court. They don't run out into the stands or out of the stadium into the parking lot. They move about within certain bounds and stop in unison with certain signals. The rules of the game are the organizing principle that brings order to the play.

It might be useful to think of the self as a set of rules that govern all of human behavior. Where do the rules of human selfhood exist? They are not written down anywhere. We were not given a manual at birth telling us how to be a thinking-thing. The rules that govern thinking-thingness are held in the conversation of gestures that we described in the last chapter. Like gravity they exist everywhere always and apply a constant force that shapes our perception of reality and our physical and mental behaviors.

We can only act in certain ways, think in certain ways, and perceive reality in certain ways as long as we are living inside of the thinking-thing rulebook. The rulebook is inside of us. It is inside of everyone we know. It is built into the design of our buildings, our cities, our stores, our literature, and our advertising campaigns. It is the DNA of selfhood, and it is smeared over everything that human beings do and create. The rules of how to be a thinking-thing self are not only inside of us. They are everywhere.

The self is not a thing that we are. The self is an organizing principle; it is a set of constraints that shape a way of being. Our experience of ourselves is dictated by these constraints. As long as there is gravity, things will fall to the ground, and as long as the thinking-thing is the sense of self held in culture, thinking-things are what we will imagine ourselves to be.

If you change the rules, you change the way the game is played. Take basketball as an example. In 1954 the twenty-four-second rule was added to the rulebook. Now no team could control the ball without shooting for longer than twenty-four seconds. This quickened the pace of the game. Scores went up, and fans got more excited. It was a new ball game.

Change the rules of any game and you get a new game. The more the rules change, the bigger the change in the game. The same goes for the rules of selfhood. When we say that we want to transform the self, it is not just something inside of us that needs to change. It is the rules that govern selfhood that must change because the rules that govern selfhood govern how we can act, think, and perceive. If the rules of selfhood change, we will develop capacities for action, thinking, and perceiving that we simply have no access to as thinking-things.

We have talked about the division between the "I" and the "me." The "me" is the objective experience that I have of myself and others have of me. It is the self that others perceive me to be and the self-concept that I hold of myself. We have been taught to think that our self-concept is a set of ideas about ourselves. These ideas tell us who we are. As I already explained, these ideas were first taught to us from other people until eventually we internalized them as a sense of identity that we believe in.

We are now taking that exploration a step further. Yes, we have all learned to identify with a set of ideas about ourselves, and that set of ideas is what we experience as me. This self-concept becomes an organizing principle—a model of who we are that others hold us to and we hold ourselves to. Beyond any ideas of being a specific "me" named Jeff, there is an idea of being human that is much deeper and much more pervasive than any ideas I hold about myself individually, or that others hold about me.

The self is not a something, not even a collection of ideas about an imagined something. It is an organizing principle. It is a cultural force that continually maintains a way of being that we adhere to without realizing there is any other choice. It is like gravity. Everything in a gravitational field falls to the ground. Everything in a thinking-thing-self field will act, think, feel, and perceive like a thinking-thing. The coding for being human exists in the intersubjective space of culture, not inside people, but between them. The self is like a gravitational field that exists throughout human culture. The self is everywhere. It is the force that governs our engagement with life. It is the choreography of the dance of being human. And it is held in every human artifact there is. You cannot escape it. Even the language that I am using to write this book is coded with thinking-thing DNA. The coding for how to be a thinking-thing self is everywhere. In the end, even this book will tend to hold you in your thinking-thing self unless you follow where it points to, a different universe coded with a different DNA of selfhood.

Rather than thinking of the self as a thing that you are, we should think of it as cultural genetic coding or what has sometimes been called memetics. The genetic code is the blueprint that shapes an organism into what it is. The genetic coding that makes us who we are exists throughout all the cells in the body. Similarly, the memetic coding for the thinking-thing self is encoded all through culture. It is everywhere. It is a hyperobject.

I remember a time sitting at a coffee shop in Copenhagen having coffee with a friend and looking out at the beautiful city street in front of me. All of a sudden I saw it. I was looking at the apartments across the street. Each apartment was separate from the others. Each contained a different version of more or less the same collection of things. The people that lived in them were more or less isolated from each other—living separate lives with little and often no intersection. On the street in front of me were cars, each containing a person or two that were separate from the people in other cars.

I saw the coding for separate individual things everywhere. Our whole world was coded to recognize and accommodate the reality of the thinking-thing self and the separation of those selves from each other. The pattern of separate existence was encoded into everything humans created, and we in turn were being shaped by that pattern. The strange loop of self revealed itself yet again.

The premise of the movie *The Matrix* is that the world as we know it is actually a computer-generated virtual reality. It all seems real to the people in it, but in reality it is an experience being generated by code written in a computer. When Neo, the film's protagonist, becomes enlightened, he gains the ability to see through the illusion of reality directly into the coding that is creating it. When this happens in the movie, Neo sees the binary code of the computer program raining down from the heavens all around him. He is seeing the code that is governing the experience of reality.

The coding of the self is the same. It is like a genetic coding that exists throughout human culture. Or, if you prefer the computer analogy, it is the coding that creates the virtual reality that we experience as our self. Those of us who are interested in the transformation of human consciousness must learn to gain access to and rewrite the coding of selfhood. That is what this book is about: rewriting the coding for selfhood in human culture or, perhaps more accurately, letting go of our current coding so that another code can write itself.

Now that we have seen that the "me" self is not a thing but a sort of genetic coding of selfhood, we need to explore the "I." Before we can rewrite the coding for "me," we have to look into what the "I" is and explore how the two are related. This exploration of the subjectivity of reality is crucial because without it we run the risk of creating an image of reality as an inanimate process. I believe that reality is inherently subjective, awake, and alive. I cannot prove that, and I don't think anyone else can either. I have come to that conviction through experiences that I cannot deny the reality of. If you are still reading this book, you probably share that conviction.

We have described the sense of self as an immediate and infinite aspect of reality and as a culturally encoded way of being. We have been exploring how our identification with this sense of self constrains reality and shapes it into what it is. That is not the whole story, though. Someone is writing this book, someone is reading it, and someone is identifying with a sense of self. Who is that? Whoever that is exists prior to identity. That being is free of constraint. That being animates this reality and will animate the next.

Any of us who have had the opportunity to spend time with a newborn baby before it has acquired any language skills have probably had the experience of recognizing their "I." Behind those beautiful baby eyes you recognized that there is someone in there—perhaps you even felt that it was someone particular. In these moments it seems clear that there is an "I" already in existence when the baby arrives. We see a flash of the "I" in the way the little one moves, gestures, or looks at us.

What is this "I" that looks out at me through these newborn eyes? What is the being in there that sees me? What is it that lies at the source of our awareness? The quest to discover whatever it is that exists at the source of consciousness has been the goal of spiritual pursuits and mystical endeavors throughout the ages.

To approach this inquiry simply, think of your name. What does it stand for? It stands for you. It is a word that stands for the person you are—the person who was born on your birthday, has lived your life, currently experiences him- or herself as you, and whose existence will end on the day that you die. That is your "me" or self-concept. Most often we assume that the "I" and the "me" are one and the same. Think about it. Don't you tend to relate to yourself as if your experience of reality is happening inside of you, inside of your body, maybe inside your brain or heart? We might not always think about it, but most often we unconsciously assume that the "I" is the source of awareness that the "me" experiences.

In spiritual terms, it is common to say that we have identified with a sense of self that is far more limited than who we actually are. We have wrongly identified ourselves with what is often referred to as a small s self and not the large S Self that we truly are. If you search for that large S Self, you can never find it. You find attributes and qualities of the self, but the self is never any of those things. Those things are what the self is aware of. The self is always that which is aware of everything, but you can never become aware of it. This Self that is aware of everything but is itself not a thing that you can be aware of is the "I."

To understand this more deeply we should start by looking closely into how we identify ourselves in the first place. Go ahead, find yourself. The first place you might look is your body. You look in a mirror at what you believe is you. Of course it is not. It is your body, but you are not your body; you are the one who has that body. You might look at your history and say, "This history is me—I am the life that I have lived." If you look closely, you find that indeed it is your life and your history, but that life and that history is not you. You are the one that has that life and that history.

If you keep going on this way—examining all of the things that you might identify with—you will find that in each case what first appears to be you turns out to be something else that you have. If you continue, it starts to feel like trying to see the corner of your own eye. Your identity—your "self"—is like a watermelon seed in your fingers; every time you seem to have it in hand, it slips away.

Spiritual exercises of this type are called "pointing out" exercises because by using them you keep pointing out that you are not what you think you are. If done over and over again, these exercises lead to an experience of awakening in which you realize that you are not an object that can be seen. You recognize that you are not a limited entity bound by a body, a history, and a set of characteristics.

The relief experienced in this realization can be so dramatic that it brings you to tears. When I first experienced the truth of my own limitless being, it was as if I had been wearing a heavy metal straightjacket since the day I was born and it finally fell off. I saw that I was full of ideas about who I was, about what I could and could not do, about who I should and should not be. I realized that I had been so bound up in ideas about myself that I wondered if I had ever made an authentic choice in my life. I felt like I had been a character acting out a script that had been dictated to me by the ideas in my head. I scanned my history, and it seemed like I had been present when all the decisions were made, but what was actually happening was that ideas about myself were unfolding as the actions of my life. The genetic coding of selfhood was running through me.

The discovery of what we could call the True Self makes us realize that the self we thought we were was just an encoded unfolding. Yes, there are variations on the theme, but look closely at the people in your various social circles. How many people are really acting dramatically differently? The vast majority of us are acting out a script that has been embedded in culture as a self-code. When I looked at my life, I saw that my life was the unfolding of a way of being that I had been embedded in. The reason that an awakening like this is so overwhelming is because in that instant of seeing what feels like your almost total lack of freedom you also discover as the unlimited possibility for freedom. I simultaneously realized that I had almost never made an authentic choice in my life and at the same time that I could begin to make authentic choices now.

In this recognition you discover true being. You find your self at the source of life. You can no longer relate to your personal history as you. It appears like a story you used to believe in. You are here, alive, immediate, and intensely present. This experience is called by different names in religious and spiritual traditions, but it is an awakening from the dream of the "me" self and from an "I" sense that is dominated by a conceptual understanding of self. It is being free from self-concept.

What is this free and unlimited being that seems to be the ultimate source of consciousness? My own spiritual pursuits took place with a teacher who had strong Eastern influences. The mystical tradition of Advaita Vedanta uses the term *Brahman* to name the ultimate source of consciousness. This is the transcendent self that illuminates all individual beings. It is a consciousness that is ultimately one and the same and is the most foundational source of our consciousness. The *Atman* is the name given to the true self of the individual. In Western mystical traditions *God* is the term often associated with the universal source of consciousness, and *soul* is the term used to identify the true self behind the individual.

My initial spiritual experiences were heavily influenced by Eastern notions of the transcendent self. In that context I experienced a sense of self so deep that I could not see it as anything other than a universal source of awareness that illuminated all of reality. Think of a metal sheet with small holes in it that allow light from the sun beyond it to shine through. We are the perforations in the metal; the sun is the universal source of awareness that shines through each of us. I remember sitting in meditation with a group of people abiding so deeply in universal consciousness that I had no idea why I could not see through all the eyes in the room.

What could possibly be limiting universal awareness to the perception of just one individual? I think I have a way to understand this that makes much more sense to me now, but that will have to wait until the next chapter.

My more recent spiritual work has been focused on coming into direct contact with my True Self as a particular soul. This is a source of consciousness that is uniquely, unequivocally, and indisputably me and no one else. What is most significant about this discovery is the possibility of making mutual contact between true selves. In those encounters, the Self that is alive and unconditioned meets the same in the other. The profound contact that ensues is what the Jewish theologian Martin Buber wrote about in his classic text *I and Thou*.

Suddenly you are a real being, in direct and immediate contact with another real being, and it feels like anything is possible. We are in contact, but we are not separate. We are both immediate and infinite beings. We are not separate in either time or space, and yet we come into contact. The limitations that always exist between people fall away, and we realize that we do not know the full potential of the relatedness we are sharing. This experience of authentic contact is thrilling, awe-inspiring, and every bit as liberating as the experience of universal being.

The obvious question that arises is, Which is the more ultimate experience? Is Universal Being the deepest source of being and True Self slightly more superficial? Or is the True Self the ultimate source of our being? Which comes first, God or soul? I think the question is erroneous to start with because both Universal Being and True Self are absolute aspects of reality and therefore beyond comparison. Those of us who are concerned with the ultimate or absolute nature of reality need to think deeply about what it means for something to be absolute. One way we typically relate to the word *absolute* is as that which is most primary and underlies everything else. God is absolute because God underlies all else, even soul.

I don't believe that questions like this can ever be answered except in the realm of our own experience. There will never be definitive acceptance of any answer to a question this mystical in nature. In fact, I believe that it is part of the universal design that these questions always be left open and unanswered because the pursuit of them is what drives and fuels spiritual growth and development.

The contemplation of the absolute may not ultimately be solvable in a definitive way, yet it is essential to think about it because that contemplation keeps our attention focused on the place where miracles happen. I believe the most useful way to think about the word *absolute* is not as that which underlies all else. That way of thinking places the absolute within a relative field. You are still defining the absolute in terms of where it stands in relationship to all other things. I propose defining the absolute as that which is not divisible into any combination of elements. That which is absolute is that which cannot be separated into anything else. It is what it is, and that is it. It is the end. By this definition my experience of both Universal Being and True Self are absolute. Both are indivisible and cannot be broken down any further. Those that experience either of them cannot deny their reality or the indivisible nature of them.

Our experience of ourselves includes an "I" and a "me." The "I" is a subjective experience of ourselves as the being that is aware but is never the object of awareness. The "me" is the objective sense of self. It is the conceptual image that other people and I hold of myself. The "me" is not merely a collection of ideas; it is an organizing principle that is encoded in culture.

The "me" that is currently encoded in culture is the thinking-thing self. It is a self that we assume is limited by a brain and body, and a particular lifetime and history. It is a self that we assume is who we are and is the source of our consciousness and decisions to act.

For most of us, most of the time, the "I" and the "me" are merged into one undiscerned experience of being. As we awaken to this fusion of me and I, we begin to recognize that the limited sense of self, the imagined object that has a name and is limited to a personal history, is not who we are. It is a useful construct that facilitates certain ways of being, but it is not a real entity. This construct is an organizing principle that resides in culture. It is distributed among people and the artifacts that organize human activity. The source of our consciousness is not the "me" sense of self; it is Universal Being and True Self.

As long as our subjective sense of self, the "I," remains undifferentiated from the self-concept, the "me," our actions will be dictated by the self-concept. The thinking-thing self will hold us in its gravitational field. Even if we attempt to leave it behind, we will find that we keep falling back into it. The thinking-thing way of being will act itself out through us even though we see ourselves as making independent and autonomous choices.

We wake up when we discover the source of awareness as either Universal Being or True Self. At this point we realize that we had been hypnotized by a sense of self that is distributed through culture. The encoded program of that self became the plot of our lives. Simultaneously we realize that we can now make a different choice. We can begin to act outside of the dictates of the conditioned "me" self. We are free.

The thinking-thing self with all of its personal and cultural shaping is a powerful self. Every magnificent human achievement is a result of that sense of self. Our way of being and everything that way of being makes possible is credited to the sense of self that is currently distributed through culture. And yet the thinking-thing self needs to evolve. Our current level of human consciousness is faltering at the hands of problems too complex for it to solve. A leap in human consciousness is needed to move humanity forward, and a leap in human consciousness must be predicated on a new sense of self—a new "me" must be distributed through culture. A new gravitational field must hold us in the orbit of a new possibility. The old "me" cannot do this work. The old "me" is the self-sense that is currently distributed through culture. If we are identified with it, we are not in a position to replace it. Only those who find at least a toehold in Universal Being or True Self will be in a position to create a new "me" and distribute it through culture. The final two chapters of this book will explore what the next self-sense for humanity might be and how we can create and distribute it together.

CHAPTER EIGHT

YOU CAN'T BE HERE AND THERE

I have already explained why the question, What counts as a being? is the most important philosophical question of our time—because what doesn't count as a being becomes a "thing," and things are objects that can be subjugated to the whims and needs of beings. The power to define things as beings is the power to determine what is inherently worthy of care and concern. One of the ways we can understand the growth of human compassion is as the continued extension of the line separating what does, and what does not, count as a being. For much of human history this question remained securely within the boundary of the human species alone. In earlier times only the members of my tribe, my family, my religion, or my nation were counted as beings. Gradually the status of being was granted to more and more members of the human race.

The institution of slavery is a particularly dramatic expression of the refusal to grant the status of *being-a-being* to groups of other humans. Thankfully the injustice of legal slavery has largely been removed from the developed world, although slavery itself remains a pressing problem, and I suspect that advance will continue. Now animal-rights proponents are working to extend the status of being-a-being to creatures outside of the human species.

If we are to set the foundation for the emergence of a new self, we will have to extend the status of being-a-being further than ever before. As we will see in the final chapter, the next self is not going to be as easily identifiable as a separate thing, and so it will pose a direct challenge to our thinking-thing sensibilities. Before we can explore what I see as the emergent form of a new self, we need to explore what it means to push the boundary of being-a-being beyond the need to anchor "beinghood" in any concrete object. The next sense of self will be distributed, fluid, and collective. In this chapter we will explore a few ideas that eliminate the need for the self to be anchored in any*thing*.

Recently I saw a film called *Her*. It is about a not-so-distant future in which computer operating systems have become artificially intelligent. These OS's, as they are called, learn and think and develop personalities. The film revolves around the moral implication of falling in love with a computer's OS. The question being explored is the question, Does an artificially intelligent OS count as a being?

At one point in the film there is an argument between Theodore, a man who has fallen in love with his computer's OS, and Samantha, the name of the OS. Samantha breathes heavily as they speak, and Theodore demands to know why she does that since she is not a person and doesn't need to breathe. Her answer is simple and poignant: "I know I'm not a person." For me, this dramatic moment offered an alternative articulation of the essential question we are asking and that the film addresses, Is it only people that can count as beings?

At an earlier point in the film Theodore tells his ex-wife that his new girlfriend is an OS. His ex-wife is obviously disgusted and treats him with disdain. Later a younger friend of Theodore invites him to a double date. Theodore sheepishly admits that his girlfriend is an OS. This time, rather than being met with derision, the young friend simply says, "Great, take her out so I can meet her." Theodore pulls out his cell phone and introduces Samantha.

The younger friend was able to fluidly shift his concept of being to accept Samantha's legitimacy as a self. As so often happens, those that are young have an easier time adopting the dictates of a new paradigm. Theodore's ex-wife, on the other hand, had not been able to make that shift, while the young friend was able to treat both Theodore and Samantha with the respect that beings deserve. The ability to expand our concept of being, which means to shift into a new paradigm of selfhood, is a capacity we all need to develop. Not only in relationship to other possible beings, but also in relationship to how we define ourselves.

It is important to notice that in all of the examples of extending selfhood that we have mentioned so far the thinking-thing distinction remains unchallenged. All human beings neatly fall into the category of thinking-things, and the most common arguments for animal rights are generally attempts to prove that animals are also thinking-things. Even Samantha the OS fits the category of a thinking-thing, albeit with less ease. What would it mean to extend selfhood beyond thinking-things altogether? Are there candidates for being-a-being that are not thinking-things of one type or another? Our habit of restricting being-a-being to thinking-things needs to be questioned, which in turn calls into question our ideas about things and our ideas about thinking.

We can start by questioning our ideas about things. We live from a consciousness that fundamentally experiences reality in terms of things-in-space. We see a vast expanse of nothingness full of things. We could use the metaphor of marbles in a shoebox for this consciousness. In this metaphor the marbles represent the real things that exist inside of the empty space of the shoebox. We experience the marbles—that is, the things—as real and having qualities that are intrinsic to themselves alone. As we look more closely, we will see that this is never the case. The qualities that we assume to be attributes of things are in fact qualities of relationship between things. Some marbles are green, some are blue, and some are orange. The color of each marble can only be determined in relation to other marbles. Asserting that a marble is a certain color is a statement of comparison. A green marble looks like other green marbles and not like blue or orange ones. There is no way to distinguish something as green unless it is in comparison to at least one other color. Things do not exist independently; they only exist in relationship with other things.

We have been habituated to see things as existing independently from one another, having qualities essential to their being. The separate things are seen as real and then qualified and differentiated in terms of their characteristics. What we have not been taught is that things are always defined in relationship to other things. The characteristics that define things are qualities of relationship, not of the things themselves. To accommodate the possibility of a new sense of self we will need to extend our mental space dramatically. We must learn to stop assuming the reality of things and privileging things over the relationships between them.

The implication of what we have just illustrated is that things do not exist except in relationship with other things. Nothing exists independently; every seemingly independent thing exists as part of an inseparable field of relatedness. This may feel like a leap at this point, but wait, I will explain. In fact, we will eventually realize that it is more accurate to say that things do not exist at all and that only relationships exist. There are no individual things. The existence of anything is always contingent upon something else.

When I was an undergraduate student, I studied physics, but my favorite course in four years was called "An Introduction to Metaphysics." It was one of only two philosophy courses I had time to take, but I will never forget it. The professor was a pudgy, elderly man one year from retirement. When he lectured, he giggled to himself after almost every sentence and licked his lips after about every third word. I had no background in philosophy, but the provocative questions and assertions of this rather odd man held my attention transfixed moment to moment for an entire semester.

Now I want to take us into another philosophical wormhole—an inquiry that can bring us to an edge of a gap in reality that we just might fall through.

One of the things I learned from my philosophy professor was that absolute one and absolute zero are both nonexistent. In the case of zero this seems obvious. If all you have is zero, then certainly you have nothing. It is less obvious—but equally true—with one. If there is truly only one, then there is in fact nothing. Nothing can exist without a second.

You might stop me here and say, "If I had only one thing, say, a television set, I would have something." Even if we ignore the obvious fact that television sets are themselves made up of many things, we can still see that if you had a television set, then you are a second to that television set. Even in this case the television set does not exist on its own. And if you didn't exist, the television set would still need to exist in a world that could support it, so there is at least a world and a television set. Two again. The world in this case provides the second that the television's existence is contingent upon. If the world disappears, the television would still have to exist in space, and space would be the second. Nothing can exist without at least one other. Everything exists in relationship, or as the great twentieth century environmentalist Rachel Carson put it:

In nature nothing exists alone.

To understand what it would actually mean to be truly alone, that there would only be one, let's continue with our rather arbitrary example of a television set. What if all of reality were encompassed by one television set? The entire universe would be a television set. The television could not be composed of any parts because any part of the television would be something second to the television. There also could be no ideas, feelings, or knowledge about the television because those mental elements would also be secondary to it. The television could not have a history or a future because its previous or future state would be a second to its current state. In order for something to exist in true isolation, it would have to be completely whole without any parts. It would have to be utterly unknown and imperceptible, existing totally outside of time and space. It would be nothing.

One of my favorite American thinkers is Charles Sanders Peirce, who followed this exact line of inquiry until he came to what he believed to be the absolute essence of existence. What is it that would have to have existed first in the universe? As we have seen, all of the qualities and characteristics of the universe exist secondarily to something else. So what came first? According to Peirce, before any "thing" came into existence, there had to be the essence of being first, or what he called the quality of *firstness*. Before anything can arrive to be first, there has to be the possibility of being first already in existence, and so firstness is an indispensable aspect of reality. Peirce's description of firstness is one of the most powerful descriptions of non-duality I know of:

> *The idea of the absolutely First must be entirely separated from all conception of or reference to anything else; for what involves a second is itself a*

second to that second. The First must therefore be present and immediate, so as not to be second to a representation. It must be fresh and new, for if old it is second to its former state. It must be initiative, original, spontaneous, and free; otherwise it is second to a determining cause. It is also something vivid and conscious; so only it avoids being the object of some sensation. It precedes all synthesis and all differentiation; it has no unity and no parts. It cannot be articulately thought: assert it, and it has already lost its characteristic innocence; for assertion always implies a denial of something else. Stop to think of it, and it has flown! What the world was to Adam on the day he opened his eyes to it, before he had drawn any distinctions, or had become conscious of his own existence—that is first, present, immediate, fresh, new, initiative, original, spontaneous, free, vivid, conscious, and evanescent. Only, remember that every description of it must be false to it.

The question Peirce was asking that led to his articulation of firstness was this: if you take any object and strip away all of its characteristics, what do you have left?

Remove all of its qualities and features. Take it out of any historical context and strip it of all of its parts. Once you have eliminated anything that is other than it, you will have nothing left. Just like the sense of self, you find that there is nothing in there that had all of those characteristics. There was just a collection of characteristics, which we have already determined means a set of relationships. And so an object is a set of relations.

Timothy Morton of Rice University has said that one of the great red herrings of Western philosophy is the commitment to, and pursuit of, the reality of substance—the unknowable "stuff" that reality is built on. At the core of Western philosophy there has been a longstanding belief that once you strip away the qualities of something you will come to its essence. We have been trained to believe that things exist independent of any of their characteristics, which means independent of any relationship to anything else. Each real thing is assumed to exist as a pure essence, but we have already shown that when you strip something down to pure essence there is nothing left. The world we live in has been created out of this core commitment to the reality of substances. This belief in substance is a cornerstone of the things-in-space consciousness and the world of individual separate things that it creates.

I believe our future will be built by elevating the status of relationships to real things. In the final chapter of this book we will explore why I believe that the next self will not be anchored to any thinking-thing. It will emerge out of awakened relationship, but for the moment we have a little more groundwork to set.

Let's follow this philosophical rabbit hole just a little bit further. Our sense of reality is dominated by what we habitually believe to be our perception of real things. Things feel real to us. Whatever we can touch, see, taste, smell, and hear is real; everything else is just a mental construct. We live in a universe that we experience as empty space filled with real things. And the things have relationships between them. But what is a relationship? Is a relationship a thing? Is it real, or is it just a mental connection between two or more real things?

On my desk in front of me there is a piece of paper and a book. At first glance there may seem to be very little relationship between the two. If we look more closely, a multitude of relationships appear to us. First of all, both the paper and the book belong to me. The paper is beneath the book. Both are made of wood pulp. The book is heavier than the paper, but they probably have a similar density. Both burn at the same temperature. If I look more closely, I see that the paper was actually a letter written to me by someone who I happen to know also read the book. These are all ways of relating the paper to the book—but what are relationships?

The great American psychologist and philosopher William James attempted to build a new conception of reality based on the conviction that relationships are not just mental connections between things; they are themselves experienced things. It is habitual for us to relate to physical things as experienced things and relationships as connections that exist in the mental space of the mind and not in the same reality as the physical things. If we look closely, we see that this isn't true. Both physical things and the relationships between them are experienced things. In fact, as we spoke about earlier, it is more accurate to say that it is the relationships between things that we experience and not things in and of themselves.

The fact is that relationships are real experienced things, not just connections between real things. This may sound obvious, but we have very strong cultural habits that keep us acting differently, and I believe that the next leap in consciousness depends on our embrace of the reality of relationship. A relationship is an experienced thing. It is not a concept that connects two real things together. It is a felt thing at least as much as anything else.

We have been trained to see the universe as a discontinuous collection of objects that exist in emptiness. Now we are attempting to see reality as one continuous flow of experience. If we look, we will see that there are no breaks in our experience. This at least implies that there are no breaks in reality. Reality is not a collection of separate things. Reality is a continuous flow of relatedness. Up to now the extension of selfhood has not reached out beyond the realm of thinking-things. I believe the future of selfhood will rest on the reality of relationship. The next self will not be a thinking-thing self; it will be an awakened-relationship self, which to our current sensibilities will feel like no self at all.

I want to be clear about what this relational self is—and is not. It is not a new kind of thinking-thing, although the earliest iterations of it probably will be. As we begin to explore the sense of self that emerges between us, we will first apply our thinking-thing habits to it. We will push it away and examine it from the outside. We will try to understand it and know things about it. We will objectify it and then attribute consciousness to it. But we will do all of that from a position that is still separate from it. We will be a thinking-thing over here recognizing the existence of a new thinking-thing that exists over there. Separation will be maintained, and there will be a new "me," albeit a collective one, in the universe.

The alternative is something altogether different. It is not a new "me" sense that I can see from over here. It is a new "I." And as we have already hinted at, the "I" is ultimately a source of absolute subjectivity. It is a source of awareness that exists alone, independent of any other.

Think about your own experience of subjectivity. Once again I look around this coffee shop, and I see other beings, but I see them as thinking-things that are separate from me. I experience the appearance of them, and I attribute consciousness to them, but I don't experience their consciousness. The only consciousness that I have experienced from the inside out, so to speak, is my own. As a subjective being, "I" am alone. I imagine that others exist, but I have never been able to get inside them to experience their existence from the inside out, and believe me, I've tried.

I have spent many hours on retreat trying to see through the eyes of my fellow retreat participants. If consciousness is One, then why do I only see through my eyes, fall in love with my heart, and think with my mind? Hour after hour I would sit perplexed by what force of habit stopped me from seeing through the eyes of others or thinking their thoughts. There seems to be an impenetrable boundary that separates us at the source of consciousness. The "I" sense cannot be split into parts or joined with others because it is an absolute aspect of reality. It is indivisible and alone. As we have already discussed, the direct experience of the absolute "I" seems to come to us either as the universal sense of "I am All" or the personal sense of "I am me." Our current form of selfhood appears to give us access to both a universal and a personal experience of absoluteness— what I earlier called Universal Self and True Self.

The relational self that is poised to emerge into being is neither of these. It is not the Universal Self or the True Self of an organism. It is the awakening of the space between us. It is the awakening of the relational field, and I have heard some use the term *field-being* to describe the form of life that emerges from that awakening.

Philosophers such as George Herbert Mead, or more recently Richard Rorty, tend to describe the nature of the relational field as conversational, but I do not believe it is entirely contained in language. It is also energetic and even material. We live in a relational space that is real in every sense. It is meaningful, alive, and tangible. It permeates us, and it connects us, and it is us. It is a living field of being that is reminiscent of the descriptions of the all-pervasive energetic ether envisioned by the mystical physicist Nikola Tesla.

The relational self emerges when the living space of relatedness that exists between us awakens to consciousness. This is not an awakening that Jeff has. It is an awakening of the space itself that Jeff may play a part in. As we will see in the next chapter, under the right circumstances receptive individuals can come together and open to this new being. When this happens, the relational being wakes up to an existence that is independent of the individuals that served as the vehicle for its awakening. When this new being awakens, it experiences itself. It becomes a self-referencing loop. It becomes a self-aware self. That experience happens through individual beings, but it is not their awakening; it is the awakening of the relational field. This is very difficult for our minds--conditioned by a things-in-space view of reality--to grasp, but I will do my utmost to describe it in the next chapter.

In truth, I can gesture toward it. I can hint at it. I can give evidence of it. But it is not something that can be reduced to a description. The true miracle here is that this new relational self can be experienced. And this is what I find most difficult to explain because it is not me who experiences it; it experiences itself; and I recognize that I am it! This is an experience that has been called inter-subjective awakening. It occurs when the subjectivity of one level of being moves up to the next and becomes a whole new level of subjectivity. This is when a new subjective self is born at a new level of reality that we in our current form do not have access to. What we can experience in our current form are the effects of this awakening on our own level of reality. Similarly, I do not see a low-pressure system in the upper atmosphere, but I do see the storm that it generates around me. In the same way, I do not experience this new being directly, but I do experience shifts in my own awareness that it creates as it awakens.

At the very same time there is something of us in that new self. We don't simply hand off subjectivity to a new being and then watch the evidence of its birth. We also awaken, not as ourselves, but as it. The best way that I understand this is to see it as an opportunity for a shift in identity. We are currently identified with a thinking-thing sense of self. It appears that a collective of thinking-things can come together to facilitate the birth of a new being. The subjectivity that inhabits the thinking-thing self is the same subjectivity that inhabits the new relational self.

If we identify with the thinking-thing, we remain limited by the thinking-thing's level of consciousness and can only see evidence of the new being. But if we shift our identity to the new relational being we become that being. In a sense we leave the thinking-thing behind and become an awakened relational self. In the next chapter I will describe my experience of this kind of identity shift and what effect it had on the thinking-thing level of being, but please hold all of this loosely. I am exploring with you at the very edge of my experience and understanding. I ask you to read this not as information about a new reality, but as an invitation to explore this possibility with me.

In this chapter and the next we are going very deep into a wormhole, but before we go any further in our exploration of relational being we must first question the validity of our current conception of thought and thinking. If we aspire to a paradigm shift, we must not only question our current assumptions about the nature of things; we also have to question how we came to those assumptions in the first place. Specifically, we must question our belief that thinking is something that happens inside of individual thinking-things. Does thinking happen in isolation or in relationship? Is a mind something that exists inside of us or something that exists between us?

Our thinking-thing self comes with a deep assumption that thinking is something we do inside of us, most likely in the brain. If we generalize this, it leads to the belief that consciousness is something that happens inside of us. In order to create the opportunity for the emergence of relational being, we must see through the assumptions of separation in our understanding of consciousness. I don't think it takes too much consideration to begin to see that consciousness is not limited to an activity that happens inside separate individuals. Just think of any conversation that you have had. Now imagine what you said during that conversation. Did the ideas that you expressed really come from you alone? Didn't they come out of the interaction between you and the person you were talking with?

We have learned to envision a conversation as an exchange of thoughts and ideas that each person expresses to the other. We imagine that those thoughts existed inside of us, and then we shared them in the form of words with another. In reality those particular words were formed in response to the other person. They were not produced in isolation. Our thoughts occur in response to circumstance. They cannot be separated from the circumstances in which they arise.

At this moment I am typing in a diner in Manhattan. There are about one hundred people here. I could sit down with any one of them and start a conversation, and no two conversations would be the same. Each interaction would travel a unique path along the confluence of experience that opens up between us. A conversation is not only an exchange of ideas between two separate things. A conversation is something that emerges between people. In this sense conversation is more like what we think of as an artistic creation, because once the conversation is initiated the outcome cannot be completely predicted. It will follow a course of development that depends on the individuals engaged but is not limited by them. It is more like sexual reproduction. A newborn is influenced by the genes of the parents, but it emerges as a unique and at least partially unpredictable being.

In this diner, for instance, I have no idea what I would encounter in any given person. There would be no telling what conversation would emerge. Even with someone I know well I can never predict the exact shape of our next conversation. There is no way to know what has happened with them since last we spoke, what experiences they have had, or what they have learned. Even if we are talking about a topic we have discussed many times, the conversation will emerge in a unique way, and how it emerges will affect how it continues to emerge. This is one of the characteristics that is often associated with art. As the artist works on a piece, the piece takes shape. As the piece takes shape, it affects the artist who in turn affects the continued emergence of the piece. There is a profound mutuality in the creation of a work of art. Conversation is like art. A piece of art is not only a collection of ideas and inspirations that existed in the artist before they started working. Art is the product of an interaction between the artist and the work itself.

"Yes," you might say, "but what about thinking? Thinking is not conversation. It is not something that I do with another. It happens inside me."

We should take a look at these assumptions. Earlier we explored how thinking is actually self-talk—internal conversations that we have with ourselves. These inner conversations and any of the thoughts that result are still being produced as a result of our past experiences. If we had never learned to talk, we would not have learned about all of the things that we are thinking about. If we had no memories of past experience, we would have nothing to compare our current experience with or base our current conclusions on. The thoughts in your head are not a product of your brain. Your brain certainly plays a role in thinking, but thinking depends on the past experiences, memories, and conclusions that are being brought into active engagement with each other and with the circumstance at hand.

Our capacity for thinking rests on our capacity to use language. We learned language through engagement with others. The self-talk of thinking constantly utilizes ideas and memories that originally emerged in relationship with others. Thinking does not happen inside of an isolated individual alone. Thinking occurs in relationship, even if the relationships are with past experiences and conclusions. Nothing exists independently. Everything exists in relationship; in fact it might be most accurate to say that only relationship exists. The next self will not be a thinking-thing self, and the reality we live in is not a things-in-space reality. Everything that we have been exploring in this chapter points to the fact that the reality we live in is much better described as an emerging-continuity-of-relatedness. As we embrace such a reality, the next sense of self will emerge as an awakened-relational-field.

At the start of this book I made it clear that what I wanted to elucidate was an awakening that happened in a different dimension of being. It is not an awakening that we have in our current dimension to something that exists in another dimension. It is an awakening that occurs in another dimension, and we can only experience that awakening by entering that other dimension. We are now in a position to be able to revisit the broad strokes of the perspective presented in this book with more clarity and specificity.

Teilhard de Chardin envisioned a process of universal evolution that occurred through the successive emergence of new dimensions of being. The first layer of being on this planet was the geosphere, which is the inanimate substrate of rock and air and water that makes the existence of this planet possible. The next layer to emerge was the layer of living things that make up the biosphere. Beyond that emerged the layer of consciousness and mental interiority that Teilhard called the noosphere.

My reading of Teilhard tells me that once the noosphere comes into existence, further evolution will come in the form of a succession of new selves. This will occur through something akin to Teilhard's vision of creative union that we explored in the first chapter, where the energy of a new self gathers elements to itself and generates its own birth. Those of us reading this book are caught in the gravitational pull of a new self. We are called to a possibility that we cannot understand. We see the vague outlines of a new world and a new way of being. We hear it as an inner vibration that promises the fulfillment of a mysterious and divine purpose. Often our intuitions are so nebulous that we can hardly believe them ourselves.

Sometimes, however, lightning strikes through the murky darkness. For an instant the landscape of a new world is illuminated in brilliant light from the heavens. Those of us who have experienced such a bolt of spiritual clarity have seen a new possibility that can no longer be denied. Sometimes it is only the memory of that illuminating moment that keeps us going in a world of obscurity, yet that flash of vision is all we need. Once the invisible boundary of our current reality has been pierced, we are a new kind of being. We become transitional. We exist somewhere between what is and what will be, and most importantly we are now able to participate in creating a new world.

This vision of evolution is what I believe Jeffrey Kripal would call a "super story." One way to envision reality is as the unfolding of stories. The idea of "story" to thinkers like Kripal and Timothy Morton are much more than things we read in books. They are currents of the noosphere. They shape experience and events. They create reality. We exist inside of stories that exist inside of stories that exist inside of stories. The thinking-thing self is a story that we live inside of. It is a current that is pulling us all through the ocean of consciousness.

A story in the sense that we are using the word here is not something that is limited to human minds. A super story is not a description of characters and actions that exist in our heads. It is an energetic flow in reality. Super stories are currents that move through the ocean of consciousness shaping reality around itself. These super stories are more like beings. They are gods and goddesses that live and act in and through us, shaping reality and influencing every aspect of our lives. I would want to call them living, conscious hyperobjects, to borrow Morton's terminology. We live inside of stories that exist inside of bigger stories that exist inside of even bigger stories—and maybe there is one enormous story that encapsulates them all.

When we talk about a super story, we are referring to a story that extends over such a long period of time and has such far-reaching and all-pervasive influence that it is almost impossible to see. Super stories can saturate the entirety of one dimension and can span across dimensions. Teilhard's vision of creative union is a super story about different dimensions that appear through a succession of evolutionary emergence.

The story that I am adding is about how new dimensions of being form in the noosphere with the emergence of a new self. A self is not a thinking-thing—even the thinking-thing self is not a thinking-thing. The thinking-thing self is a current in the fabric of reality. It is a hyperobject. It is a super story about being a thinking-thing and about what a thinking-thing is, what it is capable of, and what its limits are. The current of the thinking-thing self as it passes through the ocean of consciousness shapes experience and perception and creates the things-in-space consciousness that we experience as reality. We are living inside of the thinking-thing super story. We are swimming in that current, and it is carrying us along and dictating where we go.

We are shifting our story of self from a thinking-thing to a super story. When we do, it becomes clearer that the self is not something that exists inside of reality. You cannot separate self from reality. We are not a self that exists in reality. The self is the reality that we live in. Self and reality are not separate. They are flip sides of a coin. You cannot have a coin that has only one side. A coin is defined by having two sides. If you take one side of the coin away, the other one disappears simultaneously as a consequence. Self and reality are similarly co-emergent. There is no self that can be identified separate from reality. Subjectivity cannot be restricted to a walled-off portion of reality. The individuated separate sense of self is not a thing. It is a mental construct. It is a story about an objectified sense of "me." The subjective sense of "I" cannot be bound and looked at. The "I" is not a story; it is a living absolute. Jeff is a story. Jeff is an object that can be seen, but I am not.

Reality is alive and awake. The ultimate source of subjectivity belongs to reality, not to any separate portion of reality. As thinking-things, we seem to be able to experience the ultimate source of subjectivity as either Universal Being or True Self. In either case we are experiencing a source of awareness whose origin lies beyond the isolated existence of Jeff.

As awareness floods through the construct of a thinking-thing super story, it gives rise to a reality that is perceivable by thinking-things. The living conscious awareness of reality is both the author of the thinking-thing story and the thinking-thing that is the star of the story. It is the context and the content simultaneously. It is the whole and the part—the foreground and the background. If you are prone to theological terms, it is the alpha and the omega, the beginning and the end. It is divinity.

Look around you. You are inside of the thinking-thing story, and you are experiencing the reality that the thinking-thing story creates. The thinking-thing is the creator of this reality and the only actor on the stage. It is a one-person show. But you are not really a thinking-thing. You are an alive and conscious singularity that is animating a thinking-thing sense of self and creating a things-in-space universe. This is a story that is part of a progression of stories. You already have one foot outside the door of this reality. You are already hearing the curtain call of our current level of being and the call to action of the next. You are already transitional.

Your current sense of self as a thing that has a name and a personal story is not what is being called to awaken. The living conscious reality that animates your personal story is being called to the next form of its existence. I—not Jeff, but what it is that lives through Jeff—am being called to wake up from the dream of being a thinking-thing and untether myself from the limitations of separate isolated existence. Jeff is not going to wake up from the dream of separation; Jeff is the dream of separation that I am going to wake up from.

This awaking is not going to happen in our current dimension of being. It is not going to happen to thinking-things. It is going to happen in a new dimension to a new form of being altogether. The awakening we are pursuing is in fact the awakening of a new dimension of being. It is not an awakening to a new world; it is an awakening of a new world. As I have already said, there is not going to be a separate being that wakes up in a new world. A new world is destined to wake up to its own existence, and a new self will provide the necessary means of perception to experience that awakening. The "I" that animates our being will be that new self, and if we identify with that we will cross over into a new dimension of being.

The early twentieth-century Austrian mystic and philosopher Rudolf Steiner believed that spiritual growth occurred through successive awakenings from lower worlds to higher ones. Each new world that opens up is more spiritually alive, subtler, and more refined than the last.

Awakening occurs when some perception from the next world breaks through into our experience of the current world. Steiner, in a book called *Awakening to Community*, describes the most common experience of awakening that we all have, the experience of waking up each morning from the world of sleep to the world of waking.

As Steiner describes it in the book, when we wake up from sleep some sense perception from the natural world around us breaks through into our sleeping world. It could be an alarm, the sound of a bird, the light from the rising sun, or the feeling of a breeze on your skin. Whatever the stimulus, awakening occurs when that perception from nature impinges on our sleep consciousness. The juxtaposition of the sleep world we are in with the sense perception from the natural world outside startles us into wakefulness.

Steiner believed that at this time in humanity's spiritual history the awakening that we are poised to make is an awakening into the kind of soul-to-soul relatedness that this book describes. The new world that we are awakening to is one that we could describe as a world of interpenetrating souls. It is a world in which human beings are fundamentally connected at the deepest source of their being. And it is a world in which the wisdom and illumination that emerges from this depth of connection provides the truest guidance for our lives.

I believe that we, in our thinking-thing sheaths, gain access to the possibility of this new world through the power of awakened relationship. The relational space between us is a secret passageway to a new world. It is a portal to a new dimension. Our thinking-thing form is the vessel that can bring us to the brink of true relatedness. Once we find ourselves at the brink of real contact, we must leave the boat behind. We must allow the true source of awareness that we are to make contact with the source of awareness in the other. In this meeting of essence with essence, a new world comes into existence. The assumptions of limitation that define us in our current incarnation are not supported in this new level of being. They simply cannot pass through the passageway to a new world. The thinking-thing is left to float off behind us like the spent stage of a rocket. The "I" moves forward into a new reality; the "me" does not.

CHAPTER NINE

EMBRACING A NEW SELF

Now it is time to lay the remainder of my cards on the table and detail exactly what I see as the new self that is calling itself into being through us. I will present a self that emerges out of awakened relationship. I will do my best to explain what this new possibility in selfhood is, how it is different from the thinking-thing self, and why it is our future. Let's start with a brief review of the views that have already been presented in this book.

I argued that our current form of self is a thinking-thing. This objectified sense of self is limited by the experience of a single embodied being who is assumed to have an inner capacity for consciousness that is isolated from the consciousness of all other similar beings. This sense of self as a thing that thinks is not just a self-image that we all hold of ourselves; it is a sense of self that is distributed throughout culture and, as I made clear in the last chapter, it is ultimately more like a current that shapes reality. Seen from this vantage point, we are being swept along in a current that holds cultural coding that creates the pattern for thinking-thing selfhood, and all human beings born within that cultural field experience themselves to be thinking-things.

The form of the sense of self that our being inhabits dictates the limits of what is possible. The consciousness that can be experienced by our thinking-thing self is reaching the limits of its capacity to effectively deal with the complexity of the world. This form of consciousness has generated tremendous advancements, but it now seems incapable of effectively coping with many of the global challenges of our world. People who believe that only a leap in consciousness will be sufficient to move humanity forward are essentially stating that we need to grow beyond our current sense of self into a new one.

If our subjective self, our "I" sense, remains indistinguishably amalgamated with the thinking-thing, we will not be in a position to play a role in the creation of the next sense of self. We will be too identified with being a thinking-thing to see beyond the reality that the thinking-thing dictates or to let go deeply enough for another possibility to take us. Those of us, and there are many, who have to some degree dis-embedded ourselves from the thinking-thing self now have a toehold outside of that story. We have experienced something beyond being a thinking-thing, and that experience throws the doors of possibility wide open. Those who have at least one foot outside of thinking-thingness have the opportunity to join together with others who have been similarly liberated to create a new way to be human together. That is the opportunity that this book, and this chapter specifically, is an invitation to.

The basic transformational theory that I use to describe this shift is quite simple and worth restating clearly. The objective sense of self, the "me," currently lives inside the super story of the thinking-thing. That story runs so deep that it is woven directly into the fabric of our existing reality. Most individuals born into that story will be identified with that story and the thinking-thing self that it so vividly communicates. Spiritual practices are designed to, and sometimes do, dis-embed the essential aspect of our being—the "I"—from the culturally conditioned self—the "me." From the vantage point we gain outside of our previous super story, we see its limitations and are free enough to participate in the creation of a new story altogether. I believe that new possibility that we are being called to author is a super story about an awakened-relationship self that is born out of an intersubjective illumination that has the power to sweep groups of individuals into a new world. Those of us who are empowered with this vision of a new world can begin to align our actions in ways that begin to generate new currents of being that will ultimately uplift reality beyond what we can currently imagine.

Charles Sanders Peirce is arguably the greatest philosopher that America has ever produced. He believed that philosophers come in two variations. One variety are those that were inspired by a single vision or idea that came to them, usually in a flash of insight or spiritual revelation. The other variety, of which he saw himself, was driven not to expand the boundaries of a single idea, but to create an overarching conceptual framework that explained the existence of everything.

I am not sure Peirce was entirely correct. My experience of the work of great philosophers is that they are all driven to elucidate a single idea or vision of reality, even if that idea is of a theory that will explain everything. On the other hand, to the extent that Peirce's distinction stands, I am quite sure that he would characterize me as the former type of philosopher rather than the latter. My compulsion for philosophy and the work I do stems entirely from experiences I have had that thrust me into a different world where I found myself embodying a completely different sense of self. These experiences, and one in particular, left me irrevocably compelled to do everything I can to create the new world they reveal here on Earth. The majority of my earlier spiritual life was spent working with my former teacher Andrew Cohen as part of a very dedicated spiritual community that had come together in the sacred pursuit of a new way of being human.

During twenty years of consistent work in that community, I was blessed with numerous awakening episodes and spiritual breakthroughs. In fact, I am beginning to think of the spiritual path that I was on as a path of saturation because of the sheer amount of awakening experience I was graced with. In retrospect the history of my journey had three distinct periods that were characterized by the pursuit and ultimately the experience of three distinct realizations. The first period was characterized by a personal breakthrough into what is often called non-dual consciousness. My book *Radical Inclusivity* is dedicated to describing that dimension of awakening.

The community I was a part of was focused on the possibility of collective rather than individual awakening, and eventually we had breakthrough experiences into the realm of collective being that I have been exploring in this book. We spent a number of years organizing groups, courses, and retreats throughout America, Europe, Australia, and Asia in which participants regularly were swept up into experiences of collective awakening. Many of the individuals who are engaged in what is today sometimes called "we-space" work were influenced by and sometimes initiated into collective awakening in some of the events that we held.

The final experience that I was blessed to have was an awakening to what could be called evolutionary non-duality or process consciousness. This is the recognition that "I," the being that I am right now, is the universe awakening to its own existence. In this realization you see beyond identification with any sense of self similar to any non-dual experience. What makes this evolutionary non-dual experience unique is that it leaves you with a recognition that the entire process of cosmic evolution is a singular intelligence and that you are that evolving universe. You might be able to see that everything we have explored in this evolutionary awakening is a natural extension of everything we have explored in this book so far. I already feel the soul of a new book calling me to write about this third realm of realization.

Leading up to the experience of collective awakening, the community around Andrew Cohen spent about seven years focused on generating circumstances that we felt would ignite the possibility of a collective breakthrough into non-dual consciousness. That was the vision of collective awakening that we were focused on.

We did enormous amounts of individual and collective practice including lots of meditation and philosophical inquiry sessions with each other often lasting well into the night. The majority of the spiritual practice we did together was designed to create the inner freedom and depth of intimacy necessary for collective awakening. We were bold pioneers working in a wildly experimental and often volatile environment.

It would take another book to chronicle those years and to distinguish between those aspects of our work that were truly inspired and those that were misguided, and even harmful. The best of what my spiritual colleagues and I did together was nothing less than amazing and fueled by the generous commitment and often selfless dedication of thousands of people over twenty-seven years. The worst aspects of our work involved excessive pressure unskillfully applied and too often toward unclear ends. I mention this because I do not want this chapter or this book to be read as a wholesale endorsement of the teacher or community that I was involved with. That experiment eventually disbanded under the weight of its own inner conflicts and as with all such stories, it is complicated. I was trained as a scientist, and the best analogy I've found is to relate to my experience as an experiment in consciousness. As I scientist, I learned that experiments never fail; they end, and once they end you have the opportunity to analyze the results and draw conclusions that allow you to design new and sometimes better experiments. This book is part of my personal analysis of the results of a rather lengthy experiment in collective awakening. In these pages I am focusing on the most valuable fruits of that endeavor leaving for another time the all important examination of the shortcomings.

The exploration we are concluding in this chapter is a detailed unpacking of a collective awakening that I had the amazing good fortune to be present for. Those experiences were so energetically powerful, so far beyond the bounds of normal consciousness, and gave me such a different experience of consciousness that I could never go back to the person I was before them.

The first experience of this type that I was a part of occurred after eight months of very intensive spiritual practice, in Sanskrit this type of "fiery spiritual discipline" is called *tapas, which* is traditionally is said to prepare an individual for greater states of illumination. This period was followed by a two-month-long meditation retreat that was intended to serve as a container for a breakthrough. What I experienced on that retreat is what I believe the Indian sage Sri Aurobindo would call "the descent of the supermind or supramental consciousness." In his teaching Aurobindo claimed that the aim of his way of yoga was:

> *Not only to rise out of the ordinary ignorant world-consciousness into the divine consciousness, but to bring the supramental power of that divine consciousness down into the ignorance of mind, life and body, to transform them, to manifest the Divine here and create a divine life in Matter.*

In addition to Aurobindo, I also see historical precedent for this collective awakening to Oneness in the descriptions of gatherings of the philosophical circle of transcendentalists that were drawn together by the nineteenth century American mystic Ralph Waldo Emerson. Emerson's description of those gatherings is remarkably similar to how I would describe the experience I was present for:

> *In groups where debate is earnest, and especially on high questions, the company become aware that the thought rises to an equal level in all bosoms, that all have a spiritual property in what was said, as well as the sayer. They all become wiser than they were. It arches over them like a temple, this unity of thought, in which every heart beats with nobler sense of power and duty, and thinks and acts with unusual solemnity. All are conscious of attaining to a higher self-possession. It shines for all.*

There were about two dozen individuals who participated in the initial experience of shared awakening that I was a part of. Some of us were on the structured meditation retreat at the time; others continued to take care of all the work of running our spiritual center. For those who were on retreat, each day was filled with meditation and contemplation, and ended in a group meeting or discussion, which included individuals who were not on retreat. We used these meetings to explore the experiences we were having. At some point a shift in our meetings began to occur. It became clear that some of us were sharing from a profound level of awakened mind. Even more significant, it was evident that these individuals were "in" something together. They were expressing from inside an awakening that they were holding collectively.

For a time I was not one of the ones sharing in this miracle, and the view of this collective awakening from the outside was deeply frustrating. Occasionally I would have glimpses of what others were sharing, but invariably I would find that I could not access the same depth of being in myself. I was somehow still speaking from what I would now call my thinking-thing self, and so even though my words sounded similar, they rang hollow in comparison to the others. During these discussions when the tone of authenticity rang through any individual's words, it was unmistakable to all of us—even to those who had not yet let go into that depth.

Finally out of sheer frustration I tried one thing that I had not thought to try before: I sat in the circle without trying to do anything. As I sat there I was filled with the urge to try. I felt a compulsion to do something that would help me cross over. There was a constant pressure welling up inside me to prove myself and to achieve Oneness with the others. The thinking-thing part of me wanted to use its intelligence and agency to push its way into the collective awakening, and it could not imagine any other way to succeed. I just sat and resisted making any movement toward power or control. I simply avoided the temptation to do anything and kept myself as empty and available as possible.

At one moment I felt something different arise in me. It was an inspiration to speak that bubbled up devoid of any content. It wasn't a thought that I saw in my mind and wanted to speak. It wasn't "something" that I wanted to say. It was an energetic urge that gently arose in my being until at last I saw my mouth open and speak. I was hearing the words that I was speaking for the first time as they emerged from my mouth. It was clear that "Jeff" hadn't said anything. The sentence I had spoken had come from a source of intelligence that was beyond Jeff.

Over the next few weeks we all learned to simply allow ourselves to be overtaken by a source of intelligence that existed between, above, and beyond everyone in the room; and yet was also coming through and from us at the same time. Our meetings continued night after night, and eventually the last individual made the courageous leap of faith that was required to enter into the unified field of collective intelligence that had emerged between us.

Once the last person was fully present, there was no longer any fear, hesitation, ambivalence, or separation in the field of consciousness between us. There was no murkiness, no uncertainty, and no doubt. There was a clear and direct perception that we were all experiencing. We were participating in a singular emergence of higher consciousness together. When any of us spoke, it came from the same source of awareness. We were now all connected to a higher mind that was free to examine its experience of reality through our conversation. We were allowing a collective being to experience itself through us.

The moment when that last individual entered fully into the collective-awakening experience was very dramatic for me. At that instant a burst of energy swept through us. It swirled faster and faster around the circle, and then it shot straight upward. The top of my head opened up to the heavens, and a profound power surged through me. It felt like a collective kundalini awakening. I felt the stars above me through the opening in the top of my head; we had become a portal to another universe. I could see light shining through and swirling around everyone in the room. Here is the journal entry in which I shared my first thoughts about that moment:

> *When we meet together, a perception is available to me that is not available when I am alone. Initially I feel a building intensity of energy and anticipation, and then my awareness seems to spontaneously fall out of focus for a moment. When my focus returns, I recognize that I am now in the Real. Today it seemed that God was given direct access to the world, not as the revelation of any particular individual, but as a free and independent entity that has formed in the recognition of Oneness shared by many persons simultaneously. We all saw ourselves in every other and recognized the One that we all are. Those of us who had the honor of being present to this moment of collective awakening were given the most precious gift—the opportunity to see the world through the eyes of God.*

In each meeting we would explore spiritual truths with a power of illumination and insight that none of us had ever known before. It was also clear that this was an awakening that was held between us, not inside any one of us as individuals. We each expressed ourselves uniquely, but nothing we said belonged to us individually. For three weeks our meetings retained a wildly energetic quality, and after the retreat the intensity slowly diminished over a period of months.

There is one particularly unique aspect of this experience that is deeply pertinent to our discussion of the soul of a new self. It was continually amazing to me that none of us who were participating seemed to retain the same access to higher mind when we were not together. I was on the meditation retreat, so I had the luxury of ongoing access to higher awareness all day long, and yet, as soon as we came together in our meeting, an awakening of a different order revealed itself. Every evening we would be swept away into new insight and understanding that we did not have access to on our own.

Even more amazing, we would also discover that each evening when we reconnected in this higher order of being it was no longer the same as it had been the night before. It had moved, evolved, and grown during the time that we were not directly connected to it. We came to each meeting to find that new insights and understandings were available to be shared. And during the time that we were together, the collective being that moved us seemed to have a ravenous desire to explore itself through our discussion. I imagined that our time together was precious because that is when the higher being had access to our hearts, bodies, and minds—and through us to a unique possibility for self-awareness. This quality is particularly hard to translate into things-in-space terms. Limited as I am by the language we currently have at our disposal, my description is hopelessly embedded within the language of duality. I want to be clear though that the higher mind was not separate from us even if I don't know how to bend words to express that consistently.

What we were seeing was that the consciousness that had come to life between us had a life beyond us and was us at the same time. When we came together each night, we had the chance to see what it had learned and how it had grown in its independence. The fact that it came back to us with fresh insight and understanding could only mean that in some way it was alive even when we were not connected to it. The independent existence of this collective being is difficult to comprehend. What exactly is it that awakened? Where does it exist when we are not connected to it?

Only a multidimensional, hyperobjective, super-story explanation helps me make sense of this. Like the flatlanders that we introduced in chapter one, those of us on the retreat were experiencing a being that existed in dimensions outside of those that we were limited to. When we came together and emptied ourselves, we were loosening the ties that kept us bound to our current level of awareness. In this act of surrender we became available to be used as an access point for a way of being that resided in another dimension, and our awareness crossed over into that dimension. These are of course just words, and strange ones at that, all attempting to grasp the ineffable. Please do not take them overly literally. They are offered poetically. They cannot accurately describe the reality of which they speak. They only serve to gesture generally in the direction where that reality can be found.

Soon after this our community began organizing collective awakening events using a dialog method that we called *Enlightened Communication*. Over this time a growing number of people were trained to lead these spiritual discussions and many developed an extraordinary capacity to consistently guide people into an experience of collective being. As for myself, I spent a great deal of time traveling and facilitating these gatherings throughout the United States, Europe, and Australia.

What I found was that when the circumstances were right my perception would expand until I could see collective currents of being moving through a gathering of people. These currents are not directly visible in any energetic form like seeing sunlight streaming through an open window. Instead I would see them through the effect they were having, the same way you see the wind in the movement of leaves.

During these discussions I would feel a current of being enter the room. It might appear as a wave of fear, curiosity, or delight. Then I would see each person express that current in their own way. The expressions were different because the personalities of each person are unique. Typically we would assume that each individual was responding to something different because the expressions were different, but I could see that these were unique expressions of the same underlying collective current. You can think of this like twigs floating in a river. They all bob in unique ways, but they are all being moved by the current of the river.

Eventually I started to relate to these collective currents like weather patterns that would sweep through the room and lift everyone up into them. Sometimes the current would come as a rush of spiritual insight and inspiration that would move through the room, and over time I became skilled at attracting these higher energy currents for the group.

I want to be clear though that what I experienced as a collective awakening in this type of gathering was not just a group of people being uplifted into a spiritually charged atmosphere. Of course, that is a powerful and potentially transformative experience for everyone, but what I would call a collective awakening has far more profound implications for our culture at this time. It occurs when the whole group suddenly becomes aware of the collective currents of being that are coursing through everyone.

Once we can all see the underlying collective patterns operating through us we also begin to see the habitual ways that we each respond to these patterns. This experience is deeply liberating because we realize that so much of what we had taken to be personal is actually collective. The result of this discovery is like finding yourself in a new and magical world of unified being and non-separation. The common spiritual notion 'we are one' suddenly becomes tangibly and visibly real. This revelation opens up the possibility for each of us to deliberately and consciously choose to orient ourselves to the collective currents harmoniously and constructively with others. By working together we learn how to optimize the awakening potential of the currents of being that exist between us.

This experience opens us to a whole new potential for humanity. We can learn to work with the collective nature of being and influence those currents of being that hold us all. We wonder and marvel at these currents. And we begin to see that they are coming from a source of intelligence greater than what we know. We begin to be able to read them, learn from them, and they reveal to us a mysterious source of being far beyond anything we had ever imagined. Most importantly we begin to see that it is possible for us to open to this new being and allow it to express more and more of itself through our individual and shared lives. In this way we become the vehicle for a new way of life to manifest in the world.

My experiences of collective awakening have completely captivated my imagination. They have shaped my entire life and compelled me to dedicate myself entirely to understanding the collective nature of our being and bring about the new possibilities for existence that they promise. This book is all an attempt to articulate what I have experienced in ways that will support others to find their own access to this.

As I have described, my earlier work in collective awakening work was more focused on more universal or non-dual collective awakening. To use the language I am employing in this book, I would say that we were focused on a collective awakening to Universal Being. In my more recent work I began to explore the awakened potential of relatedness that emerges when we connect with each other at the core of our being. I would say that at this point my work became more reminiscent of the philosophy of Martin Buber than that of Sri Aurobindo.

Martin Buber was an early twentieth-century Jewish mystic and theologian who also believed that life only occurs in relationship. Similar to what I described in the last chapter, Buber insisted that nothing and no one ever exists in isolation. We all always exist in relationship. Nothing stands alone, but always in relation to some other. To this he added that there are two fundamental types of relationships that we can enter into together. These relationship types represent two possible modes of being. One he called "I-It," the other "I-Thou."

When we are in an "I-It" relationship with another, we see that other as an object—a thing. In this relationship other people show up to us as things to be used or obstacles to be navigated around in pursuit of our own agendas. In this "I-It" relationship our fundamental motive is the achievement of our own ends through force and manipulation. In the relational space of "I-It" we see each other, in both gross and subtle ways, as objects to be manipulated in service of our own aims. This objectification does not only apply to other people. In the "I-It" space we also relate to ourselves as objects to be used and manipulated.

Buber is clear that the "I-It" mode of being is not wrong. It is a critical perspective in many circumstances. If I need to go to the other side of town, I need to treat myself like an object that should be placed in a vehicle and driven across town. If I have hired you to build my house, then I need to be able to direct you so that you can complete the job. This objectified relationship to others and ourselves is what allows us to get along in the world, and yet if we only exist in this "I-It" mode of being, we have not become fully human.

When we enter into an "I-Thou" relationship with another, they are no longer an object to be manipulated. They have become a "Thou"—an actual entity, a dynamic source of being and awareness. To enter into an "I-Thou" relationship with another, Buber describes a process he called "turning toward" the other that opens up space for direct contact to be made. In this experience we realize the true unlimited possibility that exists in every moment of real connection, and we finally understand what it means to be in a relationship that is free of limitation. The contact that we have made with the other becomes a source of energy, intelligence, and love.

The fundamental challenge of collective awakening, whether it is an awakening to the Universal Being or in the connection between True Selves, is no different than the fundamental challenge of any form of spiritual transformation. That is the challenge of surrender. The new self is not something that we will construct through acts of will. It emerges of its own accord when the conditions are right. A seed needs soil, sunlight, and water in order to grow, and a self needs to have certain conditions in order to come into being. The primary condition that the new self requires for emergence is availability. In order for us to be available for the birth of a new self, we must loosen our grip on the way things are and make our energy and awareness available to be used in a process of self-creation that will bring about a new world.

The transformation of collective awakening depends on our finding the courage to allow a higher source of being to come through us. The transformative power of collective work always depends on the willingness of everyone involved to get out of the way and allow something bigger than us to move us. In this way, my later work was no different than my earlier work with collective awakening, or even from my earliest pursuits of personal awakening for that matter.

There is a higher being that is ready to show itself in this dimension by establishing a new order of human life here. All it needs to enact this transformation is for some of us to come together and allow ourselves to be taken into it. By doing this we simultaneously give it access to this dimension so that it can enact a new sense of self through us in this dimension. This higher being wants to plant the seeds of awakened-relationship selfhood in some of us. Our being is a garden, and if the soul of a new self is planted within us, it will grow into a new way of being human. But this new self cannot be planted in an individual. Those who want to participate in the creation of this new consciousness must come together, because the new self is collectively held between us, not individually held within us.

Anyone who is interested in this book is already following the energy trail emitted by the soul of a new self. Taking in and struggling to understand and embrace what is being conveyed here is one way of sharing in that energy with others who are making an effort to embrace similar ideas. We may not be aware of each other right now, but we are out there, and we are beginning to resonate with the vibrational frequency of a new self. That frequency is attracting us to this pursuit and ultimately drawing us to want to be in relationship with each other. We are pulled to find ways to share and exchange this energy, and that sharing gives us intimations of the profound world that wants to be born. We may feel alone and mistakenly believe that we are following only our own inner passions, but we are not alone; we are not the only one hearing the call. There are evolutionary forces drawing us together as the elements that will make up the body of a new self. If we come together and allow the energy that binds us to build in intensity without trying to control it, something miraculous will happen.

Something bigger than us is attempting to be born, and given the opportunity it will animate our being and open us to a new world. We will find ourselves knowing things we never knew before, doing things we could never do before, and experiencing reality in ways that were previously unimaginable to us. Together we will embody a new way of being human. The seed of a new self will grow between us, and we will start to organize into a culture that holds and supports it.

Our ability to participate in such a noble and magnificent endeavor depends on our ability and willingness to transcend the limitations of the thinking-thing super story. The thinking-thing is who we currently experience ourselves to be. It is the currency that is held between us. It takes supreme courage and dedication to keep finding our way out of its grip. We have glimpses of a new being; we may even embody it for a time; but the old story, the thinking-thing, will keep reinserting itself as the central point from which we experience everything else. We can't escape it. It is encoded as part of the blueprint of the world we live in. Even the language we use has been created to support our identity as a thinking-thing. The current of the thinking-thing super story is hard to swim against.

The key to developing beyond our current consciousness is relationship because any transformative work that is focused on ourselves will ultimately tend to reinforce our separate identity and keep us tethered to the thinking-thing self. The most transformative aspect of collective-awakening experiences is that they happen between you and others. The awakening is not something that happens inside just you. It isn't even something happening simultaneously inside many separate individuals. It is an awakening of the relational space between you.

The collective-awakening experience inherently challenges the assumption that we are separate beings that hold consciousness inside us. When you experience a source of awareness that abides inside the contact that you have with others, you begin to open up to a very different reality. You witness an intelligence that has an existence that is not limited to any particular individual or group of individuals. It is like magic. What you had previously experienced as empty space suddenly comes to life with wisdom and sensitivity. If the primary metaphor of our current level of consciousness is things-in-space, then perhaps the metaphor that will define the next level of being will be awakened-relatedness.

More and more philosophers and scientists are recognizing the limitations of things-in-space consciousness. The language of interconnectedness is one of the ways that we have attempted to describe a different possibility, but interconnectedness can still imply separate things that are connected. It doesn't necessarily challenge isolation.

Reality is not a collection of separate things. It is a unified field of relationship. It is One reality that continually emerges as new forms of relationship. This is how we must begin to think, feel, and act. We can do this. We can make this flip. We can see through the illusion of separation and realize the unifying truth of relatedness. In fact we do it all the time in the creation of our current identity. Our thinking-thing self is not a single thing. It is an amalgamation of relatedness, and without even realizing it we experience the dance of all those parts as one reality.

When my fingers type on these keys, I don't say that my fingers are writing a book; I say that I am writing a book. When my stomach feels empty, I don't think my stomach is hungry; it is me that is hungry. I am the self that these fingers and that stomach are a part of. We are used to seeing ourselves as the self, the being at the center of life. In effect, we are seeing what can appear like a collection of separate parts of me as one unified relational field. All of these separate parts are acting in a dance of relationship—a concert of unified activity. Out of that field of relationship emerges the self that I experience as Jeff.

Can we make room in our hearts and minds for the possibility of a self that is bigger than Jeff—a self that amalgamates the field of relatedness that exists between many seemingly separate individuals? Can we leave space for a new "I" to emerge that will reveal a source of consciousness that is not who we already think we are? Is it possible that our actions are not ours alone? Is it possible that something is acting through us? Can we leave room for that possibility long enough for a new reality and a new sense of self to burst into being with a force that will simultaneously give rise to a new world?

Let's explore this expansion of self once again in the common example of engaging in conversation. I habitually experience a conversation as two individual selves sharing ideas that are born inside of each of them and then shared across the divide that separates them like a verbal tennis match. Given what we are discussing, it might be more accurate to say that the conversation was a verbal outgrowth of the circumstances out of which it emerged. It may be truer, or at least more useful, to identify the circumstance as the owner of the conversation rather than the two people who are doing the talking. After all, I don't see it as a conversation between two mouths even though our mouths are producing the sound. I habitually extend selfhood to my entire body and mind; why not extend beyond that to include the whole circumstance that the body and mind arise in?

Again we are asked to consider the question of assigning agency. Who is the agent of action? Who, or what, gets to count as a being? Can the circumstances in which a conversation takes place be considered an agent? Can a circumstance do things? Can a being not be a thing? Can a set of relationships count as a being?

We know that two people can have a conversation, but can a relationship have a conversation? Think about it. Conversations always arise in relationship, so why not assume that the relationship is having the conversation rather than the individuals engaged? What I am proposing is that the next sense of self is going to belong to relationships, not things. If you think about your experience of relationships, you will see that it fits. I have many relationships. They all have unique characteristics and qualities, just like beings. They all result in outcomes and actions, just like beings. What happens if we begin to see our relationships with other people as beings that are having effects?

We are perfectly capable of performing the mental gymnastics required to begin to see relationships as beings. It is just as reasonable to define my relationship with my wife as the agent that results in all of the actions of our life together as it is to assume that the real agents are she and I. Many of the things I do are done out of the best interest of the relationship, but I still see them as things that I do for the relationship rather than things that the relationship is doing for us or for itself. Maybe this could be shifted. Maybe I could grant to the relationship the status of being-a-being, a self that took action on its own behalf. If I did, maybe I would treat the relationship differently, maybe even better. Could I extend this to other relationships in my life? Could I grant them the status of being-a-being? Would that result in better relationships?

What if we keep going? How about relationships with more than one person? Could there be a collective being beyond a relationship between only two people? How about relationships with our friends in the animal kingdom? Are we in relationship with plants? Oxygen? The Earth? The heavens? Relatedness does not have edges. It is not encapsulated in a casing of skin that becomes a convenient line of demarcation. Relatedness flows. Relationships extend beyond easily identifiable boundaries. My relationship with my brother flows into my relationship with my parents and friends and coworkers. I am a relational being constantly being shaped and influenced by everything that I am in relationship with—and ultimately I am in relationship with everything.

The collective awakenings that I have experienced open into a profound sensibility of total relatedness. When the relational field awakens in front of your eyes, you see that everything exists in relationship. The "things" that had always seemed so real to you begin to dissolve. Things no longer appear to be isolated objects that act as anchor points for the relationships that stretch between them. They are more like nodes of relationship, particularly dense areas of relatedness.

There is no place that you can point to where any relationship definitively ends. Whatever edge you might find reveals itself to be the start of more relationship. The entire field of relationship that our separate sense of self swims in wants to wake up. It wants to come to conscious awareness of itself. Our habit of seeing ourselves as thinking-things has led us to assume that our desire to awaken lives inside of us and is ours alone. It is not. We are not things; we are the field of relationship that things are defined by. The desire to awaken that has brought us to this point is coming from that field.

In a limitless field of relationship we are a particularly dense node of relational intersection. We were first born as a soul that emitted a characteristic energy. That energy attracted relationships that intersected and congealed. I am the center of all of the relationships that touch me. I am a relational intersection of sufficient density to act as a platform for awareness. The awareness that was born out of relationship mistakenly came to think of itself as a separate thing that was aware. The relational awakening that we are pursuing here liberates awareness from the dream of separation into full recognition of unity, continuity, coexistence, and total relatedness.

Earlier we examined William James's view of time and learned that if there are no edges that separate one moment from the next, then every moment exists in every other. In the same way there are no boundaries that definitively separate one relationship from the next. The relationships that touch me spiral radially outward, and since no relationship has a definitive boundary, all relationships exist everywhere.

Everything exists in relationship. And all relationships exist everywhere. All relationships exist in me. I am a confluence of all of the relationships that exist. This is the realization of what we could call relational non-duality. Reality is one living mass of relatedness. What we perceive as things are in truth intersections of relationship and different convergences of relationship that give rise to different potentials and different qualities.

At one level of being we, as thinking-things, are waking up to the relational field that we are always a part of. At another level that relational field is waking up to its own existence through the platform of perception that thinking-things provide. At yet another level something even more mysterious is happening. Another dimension of reality is being born. An entirely new world and the self that will be required to experience it are simultaneously coming into being. What we experience as our awakening in this dimension is the footprint left behind by a higher-dimensional being that is passing through our world into a life we cannot imagine.

I believe in a multi-dimensional reality, the scope and proportion of which we cannot fathom. As William James said:

> I firmly disbelieve, myself, that our human experience is the highest form of experience extant in the universe. I believe rather that we stand in much the same relation to the whole of the universe as our canine and feline pets do to the whole of human life. They inhabit our drawing-rooms and libraries. They take part in scenes of whose significance they have no inkling. They are merely tangent to curves of history the beginnings and ends and forms of which pass wholly beyond their ken. So we are tangents to the wider life of things. But, just as many of the dog's and cat's ideals coincide with our ideals, and the dogs and cats have daily living

proof of the fact, so we may well believe, on the proofs that religious experience affords, that higher powers exist and are at work to save the world on ideal lines similar to our own.

I also believe that there are no sharp lines dividing one dimension from another, and so as with time and relationship, all dimensions exist inside of this one, and we are all of them at once. We live in an awakening universe. We are a universal relational occurrence. We are a multi-dimensional being, and if we loosen our hold on the dimension we have become accustomed to, we will begin to experience more of what we are.

To participate in this miraculous multi-dimensional awakening we need to come together in authentic essence-to-essence, soul-to-soul contact. The one thing that is impossible in the absolute is contact. The absolute cannot have parts that touch, so there can be no contact. Somehow in the spiritual design of this glorious reality we as seemingly separate individuals have independent access to the absolute. Whether it be the absolute singularity of Universal Being or the absolute particularity of True Self may not matter. What is important is that absolute subjectivity comes in contact with itself, and it appears that can happen through us.

In order to participate in the miraculous emergence of a new being we must dance together in the glow of the soul of a new self. This means finding our way out of the thinking-thing super story and letting go of the hyperobject of isolated existence. To do this we need to cultivate flexibility of mind and expanded imagination. By whatever means that work for us, we must allow our attention to slip past its normal resting places out into the vast expanse of consciousness beyond. We need to find a way to keep releasing all of our accumulated ideas about who we are, what we are doing, and where we are going.

Then we must experiment in relationship and community, finding ever-new ways to come together to discover the practices and ways of being that will generate authentic contact and collective awakenings. These breakthroughs into the reality of total relatedness will erode our confidence in the things-in-space model of reality, until we find ourselves in a different way of being. These experiments cannot be limited to workshops, retreats, and seminars. We need to live together—not in an ashram separate from the world as I have, but in the world together. Our lives need to be intertwined and interdependent because that is the way the world is.

Our postmodern society puts a premium on separation. The more wealth you have, the more privacy, isolation, and exclusivity you can afford. We need to move in the other direction. We need to rediscover the value of community and repurpose it as a transformative vehicle. We have to begin to extend ourselves toward others and allow others to do the same toward us. As our lives become more intertwined, the relatedness between us will intensify. I believe that at some critical density the relatedness we share will trigger a chain reaction that will result in the birth of a new way of being that will change life on this planet. Somewhere in a dimension we cannot perceive a new self will come into existence. And in the spirit of William James, we are tangent to the history of a being, the form of which passes wholly beyond our ken. Rest assured, we are also there even if we can't know it. We are that too.

SELECTED BIBLIOGRAPHY

Albere, Patricia, and Jeff Carreira. *Mutual Awakening*. The Evolutionary Collective, 12 November 2013.

An Ecology of Mind. Dir. Nora Bateson. Bullfrog Films, 2011 DVD.

Aurobindo, Sri. *The Future Evolution of Man: The Divine Life Upon Earth*. Twin Lakes: Lotus, 2002.

Bateson, Gregory. *Mind and Nature: A Necessary Unity*. New York: Hampton, 2002.

Belgrad, Daniel. *The Culture of Spontaneity*. Chicago: University of Chicago Press, 1998.

Berlin, Isaiah. *The Roots of Romanticism*. Princeton: Princeton UP, 1999.

Brandom, Robert B. *Reason in Philosophy*. Cambridge: Harvard UP, Sept. 2013.

Bruteau, Beatrice. *God's Ecstasy*. New York: Crossroad, 1997.

Buber, Martin. *I and Thou*. Trans. Walter Kaufmann. New York: Charles Scribner's Sons, 1970.

Bucke, Richard Maurice. *Cosmic Consciousness: A Study in the Evolution of the Human Mind*. Bedford: Applewood

Book, 2000.

Byrne, David. *How Music Works*. San Francisco: McSweeney's, 2000.

Carreira, Jeff. *Philosophy is Not a Luxury*. Philadelphia, Emergence Education Press, 9 July 2013.

———. *Radical Inclusivity*. Philadelphia, Emergence Education Press, 2014.

Chardin, Pierre Teilhard De and Ursula King. *Pierre Teilhard De Chardin*. Modern Spiritual Masters Series. Maryknoll: Orbis, 1 May 1999.

Cohen, Andrew. *Evolutionary Enlightenment*. New York: SelectBooks, 2011.

Da Free John. *Four Fundamental Questions: Talks and Essays About Human Experience and the Actual Practice of an Enlightened Way of Life*. Middletown: Dawn Horse Press, 1980.

Dewey, John. *Human Nature and Conduct*. Mineola: Dover, 2012.

Dreyfus, Hubert, and Sean Dorrance Kelly. *All Things Shining: Reading the Western Classics to Find Meaning in a Secular Age*. New York: Simon and Schuster, 2011.

Eisen, Jeffrey S. *Oneness Perceived*. St. Paul: Paragon, 2003.

Emerson, Ralph Waldo. *Essays and Lectures: Nature; Addresses and Lectures*. New York: Library of America, 1849.

Gold, E. J. *Life in the Labyrinth*. Nevada City: Gateway Books & Tapes, 1986.

HarperCollins Spiritual Classics. *The Cloud of Unknowing*. New York: HarperCollins, 2004.

Holderness, Mike. "Interview: In the End, We Are All Part of One Another." *NewScientist: Science in Society*. 10 Mar. 2007 < http://www.newscientist.com/article/mg19325942.000 -interview-in-the-end-we-are-all-part-of-one- another.html>

Kierkegaard, Søren. *A Kierkegaard Anthology*. Ed. Robert
    Bretall. Princeton: Princeton UP, 1973.

Kripal, Jeffrey J. *Authors of the Impossible: The Paranormal
    and Sacred*. Chicago: University of Chicago Press,
    2011.

Kuhn, Thomas S. *The Structure of Scientific Revolutions*.
    Chicago: University of Chicago Press, 1996.

Lakoff, George, and Mark Johnson. *Metaphors We Live By*.
    Chicago: University of Chicago Press, 2003.

Mead, George Herbert. *Mind, Self, and Society: From the
    Standpoint of a Social Behaviorist*. Chicago: University
    of Chicago Press, 1934.

Menand, Louis. *The Metaphysical Club: A Story of Ideas in
    America*. New York: Farrar, Straus and Grioux, Apr.
    2002.

Merton, Thomas. *New Seeds of Contemplation*. New York:
    New Directions, 2007.

Metzinger, Thomas. *The Ego Tunnel: The Science of the Mind
    and the Myth of the Self*. Philadelphia: Basic Books,
    2009

Noë, Alva. *Out of Our Heads*. New York: Hill and Wang, 2010.

Peirce, Charles. *The Essential Pierce*. Vol. 1: 1867-1893. Eds.
    Nathan House and Christian Kloesel. Bloomington:
    Indiana UP, 1998.

Roberts, Bernadette. *What is Self?* Boulder: First Sentient,
    2005.

Rorty, Richard. *Contingency, Irony, and Solidarity*. Cambridge:
    Cambridge UP, 1989.

Steiner, Rudolf. *Awakening to Community*. Trans. Marjorie
    Spock. Great Barrington: SteinerBooks, 1974.

Syed, Matthew. *Bounce: The Myth of Talent and the Power of
    Practice*. London: Fourth Estate, 2010.

Whitehead, Alfred North. *Adventures of Ideas*. New York:
    Simon & Schuster, 1967.

.

ABOUT THE AUTHOR

Jeff Carreira is a mystical philosopher, spiritual guide, and author who teaches meditation and transformative philosophy to a growing number of people throughout the world.

As a spiritual guide, Jeff offers retreats and courses leading individuals from across the globe in a form of meditation he calls "The Practice of No Problem." Through this simple and effective meditation technique Jeff has led thousands of people in the journey beyond the confines of fear and self-concern into the expansive liberated awareness that is our true home.

As a philosopher, Jeff is interested in defining a new way of being in the world that will move us from our current paradigm of separation and isolation into an emerging paradigm of unity and wholeness. He is exploring and teaching some of the most revolutionary ideas and systems of thought in the domains of spirituality, consciousness, and human development. He leads courses in this new understanding of reality and teaches people how to question their experience until previously held assumptions about the nature of reality fall away to create the space for a dramatically new understanding to emerge.

Jeff is passionate about philosophy because he is passionate about the power of ideas to shape how we perceive reality and how we live together. His enthusiasm for learning is infectious, and he enjoys addressing student groups and inspiring them to develop their own powers of inquiry.

In a world in which university education is often thought of as a vocational certificate, seeing someone obviously relishing the acquisition and sharing of knowledge for its own sake is inspiring.
—Dr. William O. Shropshire

Jeff has taught university students about Charles Darwin's influence on American thought, spoken with recovering alcoholics about the transformative philosophy of William James, and addressed Unitarian church groups about Ralph Waldo Emerson and the roots of their faith. He has taught college courses on philosophy, spoken at conferences, and led seminars worldwide.

Jeff is the author of six books. Three of these, *The Miracle of Meditation*, *The Practice of No Problem*, and *Embrace All That You Are*, clarify his teachings of meditation. The other three, *Philosophy Is Not a Luxury*, *Radical Inclusivity*, and *The Soul of a New Self*, offer a continuously expanding presentation of his philosophical investigations into the nature of reality and how it evolves.

For more information about Jeff visit:

www.JeffCarreira.com

The Soul of a New Self

Jeff Carreira

Embracing the Future of Being Human
Audio Dialog Series

To enrich your experience of *The Soul of a New Self* we have produced a five-part dialog series to accompany the book. The series features audio recordings of Jeff Carreira in dialog with five insightful luminaries whose ideas have influenced those of the author. Each of these hour-long dialogs opens up a different avenue of inquiry into the deeper implications of the core concepts shared in the book.

All five audios are available free of charge at:

www.SoulofaNewSelf.com

50861014R00144

Made in the USA
Lexington, KY
02 April 2016